THE COACH MAKES THE DIFFERENCE

Develop Your Vision on Leadership, Talent, Motivation, and Selection

Mauro van de Looij

Copyright © 2024
All Rights Reserved

The Coach Makes The Difference Reviews

'The lessons and examples are so universal that this book is also very useful for coaches in other sports and the 17 million national coaches with a management job.'
Elly Stroo Cloeck – Reviewer 1001 ManagementBook

'A book that clearly indicates that every trainer can play an important role in the development of youth football players. With expertise, an open mind and, above all, love for the game.'
Foppe De Haan – Former Netherlands U21 Head Coach

'I wish every child a coach who deals with his players as described in this book.'
Bastiaan Riemersma – Assistant Coach FC Eindhoven

'This weekend I dug into your book... AMAZING! And I can certainly imagine that your book is very valuable for teacher training.'
Mariken van Roosmalen-Noppen, teacher and teacher educator

'This book is a basic document for every youth coach.'
Toon Gerbrands – Former Olympic Volleybal Coach and General Director of PSV Eindhoven

'Mauro makes scientific insights practical in a fun way.'
Art Langeler – International soccer coach, former Dutch FA

'Read, studied and highlighted it.. A book I love to delve into to develop myself.'
Dennis Reus – International soccer coach, former Ajax Amsterdam

For a fun and educational time on the sports field for as many children and their coaches as possible.

About the Author

Mauro van de Looij is a sport and performance psychologist. He's worked as a youth coach at PSV Eindhoven and Willem II Tilburg, he now teaches (performance)psychology at Fontys University of Applied Sciences and he coaches students, teachers, athletes, and sportscoaches. Learning and sharing insights from psychology to get the best out of himself and others is what drives him.

Contents

Preface by Willem Weijs

Introduction

1 The Role and style of the coach: who inspires players?

1.1 What is your style?

1.2 Which leadership styles are useful?

1.3 Wat do (young) players appreciate in a coach?

2 Motivation: what drives players?

2.1 Intrinsic versus extrinsic: driven by yourself or by other factors?

2.2 Autonomy: do you give your players choices?

2.3 Competence: do you look at what your players can do?

2.4 Relatedness: does everyone belong?

3 Perspective: do you believe you can?

3.1 Mindset: do you believe in development?

3.2 Focus: complete or incomplete control?

3.3 Ownership: how to create leaders?

4 Selecting players: what do you look for?

4.1 Selecting: what does daily practice look like?

4.2 Selecting: what does science say?

4.3 Practical tips for selecting

5 Sharing your vision: how to create clear expectations?

5.1 What club appointments do you make?

5.2 What team agreements do you make?

5.3 What agreements with parents do you make?

6 Training: how to improve performances?

6.1 How do you set effective training goals?

6.2 How do you align with what your players can already do?

6.3 How do you train as holistically as possible?

6.4 How can you convey skills, attitude, and knowledge?

6.5 What are good soccer exercises?

7 Coaching a match: how do you make a difference?

7.1 Wanting to win: the aim of the game?

7.2 Safety: can everything be there?

7.3 Vulnerability: can I be imperfect?

7.4 Goal Orientation: what am I fighting for?

8 How do you bring the ideas and tips from this book in your practice?

Inspiring people, book tips, and more

Resources

Preface

I feel truly honored that I was asked to write this preface. As long as I can remember I've loved to work with other people and I am completely obsessed with soccer. You could say becoming a soccer coach is a logical consequence. On top of that I try to improve myself to become the best I can be on a daily basis. That drives stems from my passion. I am convinced that if I become the best version of me others, like my players and staff, will profit from that too. More knowledge and experience means better coaching and better craftsmanship. Especially for soccer coaches these competencies are indispensable.

I know for sure this book will bring you further as a coach. I won't say I'm a good coach myself, however I am convinced I am a better coach than I was seventeen years ago when I started my internship with PSV Eindhoven Academy. Mainly I've grown because I was open to everybody and everything to learn from according to my goal to learn. I suggest you too keep your eyes and ears open so that you can learn from the situations and people around you. Whenever I see behavior that appeals to me I try to it. Whenever I see behavior that doesn't fit me I try to pinpoint what I would different in that same situation. In both cases it's about combining the knowledge with your own ideas so you can form your own vision. That's what makes this book Mauro van de Looij wrote so valuable. He shares knowledge that helps you be at your best, especially when you add your own way to it.

Because I became a soccer coach suddenly, without experience and a very limited vision I can imagine you like this opportunity of receiving guidelines, a vision, experience and knowledge. This book will no doubt present you the greatest secrets to being a great coach. Why does one coach get the team in a flow whilst another coach struggles to create a mastery climate focused on learning? What should you definitely take into account as a coach and what do you say to your team so that every player understands what you mean? If you're eager to learn these kinds of secrets then I recommend you to quickly read on. Remember that you're halfway already if you are able to develop your own vision and can convey this to your players. It sounds easy, but it comes down to that. The magic of forming and conveying a vision is not that easy though. I know for sure this book will take you a big step in the right direction. I wish you all the best on your route to becoming the best version of you and most of all enjoy this wonderful book!

Kind regards,

Willem Weijs

2023-2024 FC Eindhoven head coach

Former PSV Eindhoven Academy, Ajax Amsterdam Academy, NAC Breda U19, Willem II U23, RSC Anderlecht (assistant-coach)

Introduction

When I think back on our youth days on the sports field with my former teammates – I have done several sports, but in particular, I have played a lot of soccer. We become aware of how wonderful and educational that time has been for us. That is what I wish for every child and probably, your wish too. It is my dream, and maybe yours too, that kids who do sports now, later, have fond memories of their sports experiences during their youth and have a clear idea of what football, or sports, to them are all about. Ultimately, they think back to you, the coach, with a smile. When I started my career as a coach at PSV Eindhoven, I had no experience as a soccer coach. I also had no coaching badges. Perhaps, you are a novice trainer with no experience. Are you in the same boat, like I was then? Or maybe you are already fairly experienced, but would you like a better substantiation for what you do? Any soccer coach, certainly with little or no experience, has uncertainties and questions.

What is it all about, as a coach? What do you want to achieve with your team and players?

What are the best training exercises? How to select players for a team or match? How do you ensure that your players develop and perform optimally? These questions are still relevant to me as a coach, even now when I have more experience and coaching badges. Only now do I have answers from a clear vision that I would like to share with you.

Why This Book?

In recent years, I have discovered something. As a coach, I was looking, probably just like you, for ways to make a difference for my players. I gained experience in doing training sessions and coaching during matches. In the same period, I read scientific studies, and I learned from the experiences of famous and lesser-known football players and coaches by talking to them. If it wasn't possible to talk to those men, I read their books, listened to podcasts or watched a documentary about them. That gave me a lot of new insights.

In doing so, I discovered how coaches make a difference, and It was different than I expected. Exemplary for that discovery is what I learned about Sir Alex Ferguson. He was the manager of Manchester United, one of the largest Soccer clubs in the world. In a period of around 25 years under his spell, United became national champion thirteen times, won the FA Cup five times, won the Champions League twice, and twice the world cup for club teams. How did Ferguson do that? Van Nistelrooij told me, "He (Ferguson) never talked about tactics with us (the players)."

The Other Side of Training

A good soccer coach has football know-how. He knows the tactics, has good training exercises, and is aware of the football trends. That's how we see the coach. Just look at the coaching badges courses, at least in the Netherlands. During these courses, you learn to devise the best training exercises for every level and make match analyses and annual plans. In addition, the internet is full of websites for soccer coaches. These websites offer the best training exercises, match tactics, and the latest match analyses. That specific soccer know-how is important to a coach.

But do you make a difference for your players with that know-how? Just think back to the coaches you have had yourself. How did your favorite coach differ from others? Was it the technical

Introduction

knowledge, one particular exercise, or the match tactics, or was it something else?

I have discovered that for most players, their favorite coaches make the difference in another way. This concerns things such as: How does a coach react when his player makes a mistake? How does a coach motivate his players? Does the coach contribute to his players' self-belief? Does a coach show interest in the person behind the player? How does a coach, coach his players? The way the coach interacts with his players is how he makes a difference. That is how coaches differ from each other, I found. And with that, your favorite coach probably made the difference for you.

In summary: most coaches make the difference in the way they interact with their players. So did Ferguson. He was a real people manager.

"Ferguson knew perfectly how to deal with his footballers," the Portuguese soccer player Nani tells Tribuna Expresso. "He always felt how he could best guide us professionally and humanely. Thanks to him, I have had some unique experiences."

In this book, I want to talk about how you interact with your players, mostly children and young people. How do you respond to the motivation of your players? How do you get and keep their attention? How do you create a bond with each other and within the team? Of course, it is also about how you deliver training sessions and coach the team during the match. In short, this book is about how you can connect with your players and how you can pass your knowledge and experiences on to your players. This makes sure that they have fun playing soccer, learn and become better soccer players. In other words, this book is about how you can make a difference for your team and every single player.

Sharing Experience

I believe my experiences can help you answer these kinds of questions and to make a difference for your players. Why do I think so? Let me tell you.

From an early age, I have had a passion for Soccer and understanding and helping other people. On my thirteenth, fourteenth, and fifteenth, I played soccer in the youth academy of FC Eindhoven. Later I went to study Child and Adolescent Psychology at the University of Utrecht. In my bachelor's research, I investigated the effectiveness of different types of compliments on the behavior of children with behavioral problems. After that, I studied Sports and Performance Psychology at the University of Amsterdam. In my master's research, I looked at the role of mindset on learning and performance within PSV Eindhoven's youth academy. In 2014, after my studies, I co-developed the PSV FUNdament program, which at the time was very innovative.

Then I started there as a youth coach. After that, I worked for Willem II's youth academy for two seasons. Again, as a coach but I was also responsible for youth scouting, talent development, and culture. In July 2020, I made a switch, and since then, I have been teaching psychology at Fontys HR and Applied Psychology. Besides teaching, I have been involved in a cool project in which we conducted research into study success and supervision. In Soccer, I have been active at V.V. DBS Youth Under 19, have got my UEFA C and UEFA B licenses, and soccer players come to me for personal coaching.

Theory in Practice

For years, I have been able to test the scientific insights regarding learning and performance, which I gained in my studies

Introduction

on the soccer pitch. With experiences ranging from recreational teams to the highest youth level in the Netherlands. Because of this, I have developed a vision on education, training, and development. In addition, I bridged the gap between science and practice. On the soccer pitch, you do not always have time to think about what you say or how you behave. You do what your intuition gives you, and often that is good, but certainly not always. By acquiring knowledge, thinking about your role as a coach, and gaining experience stimulates your intuition, so that you unconsciously say and do the right things on the pitch, allowing you to connect with your players.

In This Book

In this book, we will first discuss your leadership. What is your style of leading? What does coaching entail? What do you stand for? You learn to answer these questions for yourself in chapter 1. In chapter 2, we look at managing your team and the individual player. How do you motivate your team and players? I believe in the power of intrinsic motivation. What I strive for is that players play as much as possible from their own drive, and I don't have to push them ahead. I primarily teach practical tips and tools for motivating your players. In addition, I strongly believe in mindset. How does a player view things? What is his perspective? What beliefs does he have? Which mindsets help him in the process of learning and performing, and which ones do not? How can you change those mindsets of players? See Chapter 3. You will also discover in this chapter what you and your players can best focus on. In chapter 4, I will discuss the selection of players for your team and match selection. How do most trainers do that? I will use scientific insights to answer questions such as: what is talent? Once you have the players in your club and in your team, in what kind of performance and learning culture do you want to work with them? Making appointments with the club, your team, and their parents is central to Chapter 5.

When your ideal culture is clear, we go to the pitch. In chapter 6, I will give you direction for organizing and giving your training sessions. You get handles in the form of didactical principles, enabling your training session to run smoothly, so that you and your players learn, perform, and have fun during your sessions.

In this chapter, you will also find a number of soccer exercises that work well in my experience and underline my vision. In matches, you would like to see what you are working on during the training sessions. In Chapter 7, you get tools to help your players as well as possible to guide and coach them during matches. Chapter 8 is about putting the ideas from this book into practice. Then follows a chapter about the books and people who have inspired me. Do you need more information or training exercises? You will certainly find several concrete starting points here.

Finally, you can see which sources I used. In this book, I refer occasionally to inspiring videos. You can find the overview of all videos in this book on my website:

https://www.bauer-vandelooij.nl/bijlage-boek.

Even after the release of this book, I will keep adding inspiring examples here.

Football Is For Everyone

For the sake of readability, I have made a choice in this book to write "he" where you could also read "she". Because the youth players I trained are mainly boys, many examples from my own practice are about them. Also, I use a lot of male football players and coaches as an example, as many readers will know them. Unfortunately, most female top players (at the moment) are less well-known. That could give the impression that I regard soccer as a men's sport. Nothing is less true. I would urge anyone who likes it to play soccer. I am convinced that everyone - regardless of gender, age, intellect, or origin - can become a better soccer player.

Finally

The knowledge and experiences I share with you, works for me in my practice. I continuously improve my way of working through the knowledge and experiences that I keep on getting. At the same time, it remains my way, not 'thé' way. Just like you, I strive to be a good coach. There are several ways to be one. With this book, I hope to get you thinking about that. Ultimately, only you, yourself, decide what to do with the knowledge and experiences from this book.

With my examples, I could give you the idea that getting players in the first team is the sole purpose of youth soccer. That can be a goal, certainly. Ideally, at the highest level, in the national team, one of the few sports teams that can fraternize a nation in such a way. But I think another goal is as least as important. That is to develop children by playing sports, in this case by playing soccer. They learn skills while playing soccer that will help them for the rest of their lives, such as working together, pursuing goals, and persevering.

In addition, soccer or sports, in general, stimulate a fit and healthy body and friendships. The most important thing about playing soccer or exercising is having fun. Fun in football brings energy, with which future generations can be inspired.

The Coach Makes the Difference

Eindhoven, November 2023,
Mauro van de Looij

CH#1

THE ROLE AND STYLE OF THE COACH

Who Inspires Players?

Being a good coach is giving everything you've got. By doing what feels good and following your intuition, you will come a long way. To really make a difference as a coach, it's useful to be aware of your managing style. In this chapter, I'll take you along the styles of four world-famous coaches: Louis van Gaal, Pep Guardiola, Jürgen Klopp, and Guus Hiddink. You discover which style suits you and whether your style suits your team.

> If your actions inspire others to dream, learn more, do more and become more, you are a leader

Simon Sinek

The Coach Makes the Difference

Being a good coach is giving everything you've got. By doing what feels good and following your intuition, you will come a long way. To really make a difference as a coach, it's useful to be aware of your managing style. In this chapter, I'll take you along the styles of four world-famous coaches: Louis van Gaal, Pep Guardiola, Jürgen Klopp, and Guus Hiddink. You discover which style suits you and whether your style suits your team.

There is a team that appeals to the imagination of many people. Everywhere they go, people along the field start whispering to each other. The scope of these conversations is their awe for this team's spirit. Teammates help and coach each other, and they cheer together as one team. They are the realization of the definition of 'team' in the dictionary. Until suddenly, something changes. The team is no longer a team. It no longer works together, and teammates are blaming each other, the cheering has stopped. The whispering along the field is no longer about the team spirit, but precisely about the lack thereof. What has changed? The coach.

As a coach, you are the leader of a team. With your words, behavior, and body language, you steer a group of players consciously and unconsciously. How you deal with success, failure, difficult situations, conflicts, and other people, affects how your players behave. Especially in times of uncertainty, people tend to look at each other and, especially at their leaders on how to behave. You are a role model for your players, whether you like it or not. As a coach, you bear responsibility, and you play a certain role in your player's life.

This, sometimes involves doubts, which every coach occasionally has. These doubts keep you on your toes. In addition, they remind you of your wish to fill in your role as a coach properly, which is a great starting point. If you stop doubting, you should start worrying. It could be a signal that you are saturated as a coach. Are you, then, still in the right place?

It is also part of the deal that you do not get along well with every player. You were shaped by your parents, their genes, as well as their upbringing, your friends, your coaches, your teachers, and the courses you have enjoyed. In short: you've been formed through all the experiences you have gained. This also applies to your players. Those experiences are why you have a better relationship with some players than with others. That's fine. Do give each player the attention he needs no matter what relationship you have with him. A good connection does not mean that you are a friend to your players, though. It is nice when they like you, but being friends with your players is more often not helpful in the process of learning and performance.

With soccer or sports in general, come emotions. Just like your players on the field, you have emotions in your role as a coach. With your body language, you radiate consciously or unconsciously what you feel, and you cannot hide your emotions. So don't try to hide them, but be authentic and show them to your players. In worst case, you express yourself incorrectly or too hard, and you can come back to that later. In the best case scenario, your players understand your emotion, adjust their behavior if necessary, and you have lost your emotion. Your players will also learn that it is okay to express feelings.

Being a coach is a craft that evolves with experience. You develop yourself over the years, and for many coaches, experiences make them a better coach. You don't have to be able to do or know everything right away. Give yourself time and space to learn. As a coach, you lead a group of players for whom you want the best. It helps you if you are aware of your leadership style and how you can best connect it with your players.

Most importantly, it is for you to realize that you really can't go wrong as a coach. You always do well. Your players feel that you love interacting with them, or maybe soccer gets you enthusiastic, and your players feel that, or perhaps, both. That is worth a lot as well. Being a coach or interacting with young people is not an exact science. There are often several solutions to one problem. Do what feels good and follow your intuition. Stimulate your intuition by experiencing and listening to other coaches, and improve your knowledge about education and training.

CH#1 - The role and style of the coach

1.1 WHAT IS YOUR STYLE

"You better go under with your own vision than with the vision of another."

-Johan Cruijff

What do Guardiola, Klopp, Hiddink, and Van Gaal have in common? They all have won a European club prize, the Champions League or its predecessor. But to what extent did they win it in the same way? Did they train, have their teams play, and guide their team and players in the same way? I have my doubts. I think they each have their own way, and several of which can lead to success or to failure. Klopp has more often not won a prize as a coach. Also, the other three coaches have had seasons without a prize or championship. They were sometimes even fired.

Scientists have written books about leadership styles and which style would be best. Partly, because of the above, I do not believe that one leadership style is best; that one strategy works for every group of players, at every club, and in every culture. I do believe in a match between the style of a coach with the player, group, and club. To have a match, it is important first that you know what your style is. What is your unique way of playing soccer, doing training sessions, managing, coaching, and dealing with people? Therefore, here are some questions to think about. What's your view on the following matters?

- ❖ What have you learned from your coaches, teachers, and coaches regarding leadership?
- ❖ What is your style of dealing with others? How do you manage others?

- ❖ What is your definition of learning? What role does motivation play in this? And talent? How do you think performance comes about?

- ❖ What kind of people inspire you and why? What do you find important in dealing with others? What do you stand for?

- ❖ What do you want to achieve with your team and players individually? What impact do you want to have on your players?

- ❖ Finally: they sometimes say a team is a reflection of the coach. What would you like to see in your team?

These questions have no right or wrong answers. Every coach has his personal way of thinking and doing. That way of thinking influences how they interact with players. What is your way?

1.2 Which leadership styles are useful?

"You can't force your will on people. If you want them to act differently, you must inspire them to change themselves."

-Phil Jackson

Scientists, Hersey and Blanchard, describe four leadership styles, which I think are very helpful: instruct, explain, participate, and delegate. Of course, a coach uses - often unconsciously and dependent on the situation - all four styles, but each coach has a preference for one style. I have linked a coach to each style, which is probably his dominant style based on his appearance, documentaries, and stories about him.

The instructive leadership style is characterized by a dominant coach. This coach directs his players by telling them how and what has to happen. That style suits players who need steering. This tactic also works well with inexperienced or relatively incompetent players. The coach that fits this style, in my opinion, is Louis van Gaal.

Josep (Pep) Guardiola is a coach who seems to fit the second leadership style: explain. Coaches with this style know, just like the previous style, what and how they want it, but they also like to explain to the players why. This style suits players who need guidance and knowledge but also have an opinion of their own. This style also works well with players who still have to learn a lot and be somewhat motivated. Coaches who prefer one of these two styles, usually have a lot of technical and tactical expertise. They are experts in soccer.

The third leadership style involves coaches who want to inspire their players by involving them in the plan. This type of coach provides frameworks and freedom. For example, this is our way of playing, this is the situation, and what are we going to do to achieve our goal? This seems to be the most dominant style to fit – Jürgen Klopp. Coaches with a participatory style want to inspire and fit well with players who are highly motivated, whether they are experienced or somewhat competent.

Guus Hiddink is a coach who fits the fourth and final leadership style: delegate. Delegating suits well with players who are highly motivated and highly competent. They are able to work more independently. A coach with this style monitors the goals and assists the players throughout the process. Coaches with a preference for these last two styles, especially, have a lot of knowledge of people. They are experts in coaching and strike a chord within the players they work with.

Of course, every coach uses – Van Gaal, Guardiola, Klopp, and Hiddink inclusive – any leadership style in various situations he faces. In fact, the top coach stands out because he masters all styles and uses the right style for the right player at the right time. One player needs a different approach than another player. And, of course, a coach does not consciously think about which style to use as one of his players asks him a question during training. But it is nice if your (preferred) style matches the players you work with. In fact: it creates confusion and frustration if your leadership style doesn't match. Every player, every group of players, every club, every culture, and every coach is different. The degree of your success as a coach, whatever your definition of success is, lies partly in the match of your style with the team and club you have chosen to work with.

A coach can change styles over time, by the way, so that it continues to match what his team needs. Maybe he starts with the instructing style, but he delegates by the end of the year more because the team has developed in such a way that that style is better and suits him. Toon Gerbrands, who has worked with Van Gaal, told me that this is how he works. At first, every player executes what Van Gaal wants, and if that is the case, Van Gaal gives his players little by little more control. A nice process that could also be your practice.

> In matters of style, swim with the current. In matters of principle, stand like a rock

Thomas Jefferson

CH#1 - The role and style of the coach

My style also differs per player, and according to every context I have experienced. During my time at the youth academies of PSV and Willem II, I used all four styles, but I mainly worked in a participatory and delegated way. With DBS, a grass-roots club, I also use all four styles, but I use 'explain' most of the time. This had to do with the intrinsic motivation and game understanding of the players, I suspect. These are relatively more present in players in the academies of professional academies than in the U19 players of this grass-roots soccer club. Obviously, these differences are relative, and they can differ per club and per player.

Ultimately, at DBS U19, during the season, I used the participating and delegating styles more often. Because every player and every team wants their own choices on and off the field, provided they are able to do so. I estimate each time how much freedom each player on my team can handle and give him that degree of freedom. With the right guidance, I am convinced, you can teach every player the skills so that he can make his own choices and becomes independent on the soccer field and beyond. Finally, it's all about the players and their independence; after all, they are the ones who play.

According to Harvard Business Review (HBR), a shift in leadership takes place in business. Because the world changes so fast, the manager no longer has all the answers, but he is most effective when he listens to his team members and coaches them. In this way, he enables his team members to work independently and perform. According to HBR, the manager of the future is more a kind of coach.

Dealing with players from grass-roots or professional academies' players is not such a day-and-night difference as people sometimes seem to think. Those players are much more alike than you might suspect. Of course, there is a difference in quality. Players in a professional academy generally play on a higher level. But, just like with team-mates from grass-roots, there can be significant differences in traits or characters within a team. A team from a professional academy has one best player and one worst player. There too, are players with motivation problems, players who have difficulty understanding the game, are insecure, get angry with other players, dislike the qualities of another player, need attention, need to learn to work together, you name it. Both at an amateur level and at a professional level, you, as a coach, lead a group of children who work together playing football.

1.3 What do (young) players appreciate in a coach?

"They may forget what you said, but they never will forget how you made them feel. "

-Carl W. Buehner

What do players actually like about trainers? How important is your bond with them? Studies in schools have shown that the bond between teacher and student predicts motivation, achievements, and expectations of future relationships within children. In 2018, researchers from Australia asked children about their teachers: "What do you value in a teacher and what not?" All children, including the ones with so-called disruptive behavior, were unanimous in their answers. They don't appreciate a teacher that behaves unfairly, unreasonably, or hostile. Think of a teacher who is overly angry for a minor offense, always picking the same child or yelling at children.

The teacher that is present for the student, listens to the student, and makes jokes every now and then, is the favorite. Teachers who behave kindly, caring, and with humor are appreciated by children. It is striking that only 10 percent of children say they value a teacher for effective teaching.

Chances are, your players will find the bond they have with you important and perhaps even more important than your soccer knowledge and training sessions.

This ties in with what some top managers, such as Guardiola and Klopp, say. They state that running a soccer team does indeed consist of leading training sessions, devising tactics, and deciding on the line-up. But the most critical aspect of being a coach, they find, is dealing with players. A coach gets to know the player and the person behind the player so the coach understands him and can help him get the most out of himself.

> When Jacco Verharen spoke with me about leadership, he shared another insight. Verhaeren used to be a swimming coach and a rather successful one. He went to 5 Olympic Games, where the likes of Pieter van den Hoogenband, Inge de Bruijn, and Ranomi Kromowidjojo were his pupils, amongst others. Verhaeren told me it's key for a player to flourish that he has a belief in his coach. Verhaeren became aware of this, especially since he made the switch from being a coach to being a technical director a couple of years back. According to him, the chemistry between a coach and his player(s) is vital for well-being, development, and ultimately results. Various research done with teachers, psychologists, but also with sports coaches have confirmed Verhaeren's insight. The relationship between a coach and his pupil appears to be crucial. The belief the pupil has in his coach plays a vital role herein. It has been shown that the chemistry in a relationship between teacher and student, between psychologist and client, and between coach and player increases the chances for teaching, therapy, and sports programs to be effective. In fact, it's a precursor for success in your player's development, performance, and results.

CH#1 - The role and style of the coach

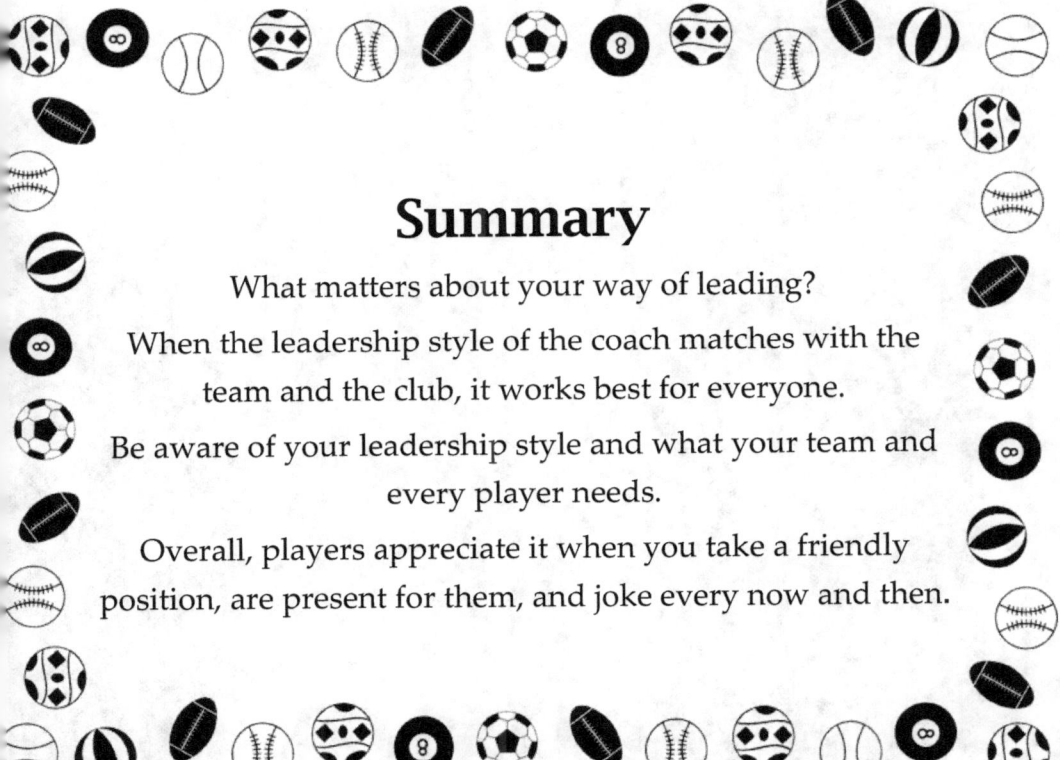

Summary

What matters about your way of leading?

When the leadership style of the coach matches with the team and the club, it works best for everyone.

Be aware of your leadership style and what your team and every player needs.

Overall, players appreciate it when you take a friendly position, are present for them, and joke every now and then.

CH#2
MOTIVATION

What Drives Players?

MOTIVATION is critical for good performance and growth. As a coach, you can undermine motivation but also stimulate it. In this chapter, I will tell you all about motivation and what you, as a coach, can do. What you want to achieve is that the players themselves want to learn and perform because in that state, they are fired up.

Autonomy, competence, and connection are the keywords.

> **Choose a job you love, and you will never have to work a day in your life.**

Confucius

2.1 Intrinsic vs Extrinsic Motivation

- Driven By Yourself Or By Other Factors?

"If you want to build a ship, don't drum up the men to gather wood, divide the work and give orders. Instead, teach them to yearn for the vast and endless sea."

- Antoine de Saint-Exupery

Motivation is why you do the things you do. It is your pursuit that drives you to certain behavior. Hunger is a motivation to eat normally. When you are tired, you are driven to go to sleep. You speak to another person about his behavior because you do not like that behavior. If you are driven to a certain goal, then you are motivated. A person who is not driven or has no inspiration is amotivated. Why are you reading this book? The answer to that question is your motivation.

Richard Ryan and Edward Deci, experts on human motivation, distinguish between two types of motivation. The simplest form of motivation is doing something because it gives you pleasure. You are looking forward to it. You play soccer because being on the field kicking a ball gives you a pleasant feeling. You bake pies because you like doing so. You run because running makes you feel good. That is intrinsic motivation. You are driven by yourself to certain behavior.

Motivation becomes extrinsic when the reason why you are doing something lies outside yourself. You are driven by external factors. For example, you get money to run. That money makes you feel good, but without that monetary reward, you wouldn't run. Or, you do homework to avoid punishment. This will not apply to everyone and every subject, but it is an example of extrinsic motivation. Basically, the purpose of homework is to "learn". Other examples of extrinsic motivation are doing things out of pride, shame, or guilt, for a higher purpose, or because it suits who you are. A student, who is working together in a group with other students, is not that motivated to work on the group project but does so anyway because when he doesn't, he feels guilty towards his fellow students. Players often are not too enthusiastic about fitness training, but they do their best because better fitness contributes to better soccer performance. Endurance training serves a higher purpose. The last kind of extrinsic motivation is that you do things because it suits who you are. You change a baby's diapers because you are his father.

Do you want players on your team to be driven because of factors outside themselves, say, by you or by their parents? Or do you want your players to come and play soccer driven by their own motivation? To answer that question, you need to know more about the effects of the two types of motivation.

Extrinsic motivation can work in the short term. However, many studies have shown that intrinsic motivation has a stronger and longer-lasting effect on learning and performance.

- *People who are intrinsically motivated, learn and perform better than people who are extrinsically motivated, in general.*

Change Motivation

Can you change people's motivation? Can you change your players 'motivation? For sure, the story of a psychologist in the United States proves that. This psychologist had some trouble with children hanging around his house. This group caused noise and mess. Using a special approach, the psychologist was able to get the youngsters away from his house. He shifted the group's motivation from intrinsic to extrinsic. Then he took away the extrinsic motivation. What exactly did he do?

Whenever the group of young people hung around his house, he gave them money. He reduced the amount of money every time until he gave them no money at all. From that moment on, the youngsters stopped coming. At first, the group hung around the house they chose. By rewarding them with money, the psychologist changed their reason for being there. Their motivation was no longer intrinsic but became extrinsic. The danger of extrinsic motivation is that it depends on a factor outside of yourself. When that factor disappears, so goes the motivation. That is exactly what happened when the psychologist stopped giving them money. The extrinsic stimulus disappeared, and with it, the reason for the youngsters to hang out in that neighborhood.

Shifting motivation from intrinsic to extrinsic is not necessarily an improvement. A similar situation sometimes arises in soccer. Maybe you know the well-meaning grandpa who wants his grandson to do well and encourages his grandson by giving him one euro for every goal he scores. You now know the danger that lurks.

Fortunately, it is also possible the other way around that you shift motivation from extrinsic to intrinsic.

Intrinsic motivation appears to be based on three needs: autonomy, competence, and connection. Intrinsic motivation is the basis on which I strive to work. You can increase the intrinsic motivation of your players. The following example from my practice illustrates this.

The coaching agency Bauer & Van de Looij, half of which is me, got an assignment to motivate a youth team that couldn't be bothered to do anything during soccer training sessions. Our approach focused on the three needs: autonomy, competence, and connection.

Prior to the training, we were introduced to the players, and we made team agreements together. Within minutes we knew the name of each player. We knew his favorite club and favorite player.

We came back to this in our coaching during the training session. Occasionally, we accidentally called a player by the wrong name. With a smile on our faces, we acknowledged our mistake and asked the player for the right name. When making team agreements, you don't need half an hour, you can do this in a few minutes. Among other things, we made an agreement with players about how many people can speak at a time.

"Suppose you want to ask or say something. How would you want the others to behave?"

Pretty soon, the players came up with their answer,"One person talks, and the others listen."

Perfect! We agree on that.

During the training session, we called the agreement when it was adhered to,"Fantastic that everyone's listening while I explain the exercise."

But we also called it when the agreement was broken, "I think someone has forgotten one of our appointments. Who can help him remember."

Partly because of this, players started correcting each other. After all, the agreement was clear and invented by the players themselves.

In the training session, we did relatively simple exercises. We sometimes adjusted an exercise so that it better matched the level of the players. In every exercise, we used goals so they could score goals, because often players like scoring goals the best. In addition, players could set their own goals. You can turn even the most boring exercise into a spectacle. This was shown in a pass-and-kick exercise without resistance. Normally, I am not a fan of exercises without resistance, and without opponents, but this exercise matched the level of the players. In this variant, players could also score points.

We played several rounds of three minutes. The players were allowed to determine together how many goals they would score in the upcoming round of three minutes of play. When the goal was reached, we set a new, higher goal. Per round, the players scored more goals. It was a party. At the same time, we made the players aware of the role of training in scoring more goals. Finally, we complimented players for behavior that we appreciated, such as trying something, improving, or just being involved in the play.

We called that behavior, "How cool that you are trying to do this or that skill."

Behaviors we found undesirable, such as shooting away a ball out of frustration, we ignored as much as possible. The overall approach led the coaches to no longer recognize their players. The players were "fired up".

The Coach Makes the Difference

Getting and keeping your players intrinsically motivated is probably something every coach wants. But how do you do that?

Players that give hundred percent of themselves in attacking, defending, and transitions. Players that explore and push their own limits. Those aren't things you do once at the start of the season, and then you no longer have to look at it. Motivating your players intrinsically is what you do all the time. What you do, what you say, what you convey with your body language, everything influences it. Continuing to motivate players intrinsically can be quite difficult because the dividing line between striking a chord or missing it is paper thin. I sometimes get it wrong; what coach doesn't? To make sure you strike the right chords in your players more often, it helps to know more about intrinsic motivation. How can you meet those three needs so that you increase the intrinsic motivation of your players?

- *As a coach, you can stimulate the intrinsic motivation of your players.*

CH#2 - Motivation

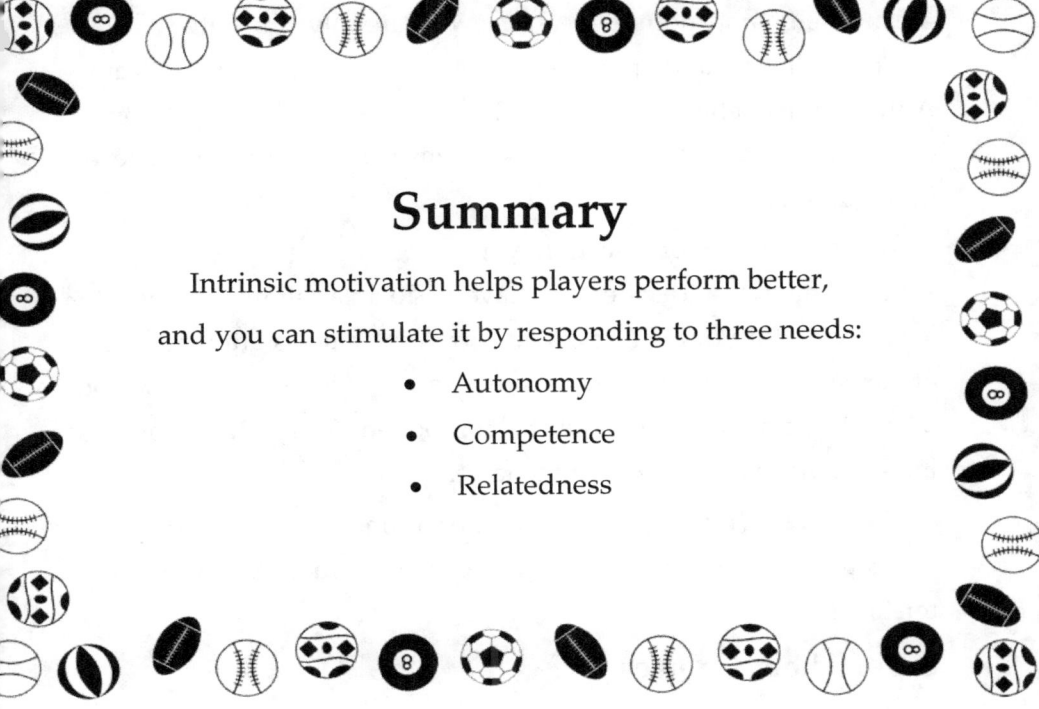

Summary

Intrinsic motivation helps players perform better, and you can stimulate it by responding to three needs:

- Autonomy
- Competence
- Relatedness

2.2 Autonomy

- Do You Give Your Players Choices?

"You can lead a horse to the water, but you can't make it drink."

-Ernst Rothkopf

Autonomy comes from the Greek word 'autonomos'. Auto means "self," and nomos means "law". Literally translated, 'ruled by own laws' and popularly, 'behave the way you want'. Autonomous behavior is behavior that is in accordance with one's own standards and values. It is a sense of freedom, a sense of independence.

In the summer, on vacation, you choose where to go. What you eat for dinner, you decide. You have to do an assignment at work? You decide for yourself how you carry out that assignment. These are examples of autonomy. You choose what you do and how you do it. Autonomy is probably the component with which you can increase intrinsic motivation the fastest.

What can you do to increase the autonomy of your players? Offer them choices, let them judge, and let them try and make mistakes.

Offer Them Choices

When your players play, you see enough points to improve. It's your job to help them improve their skills and performance. Therefore you coach them. You can do that in different ways. One way is that you instruct your players from A to Z on how and what to do, and you might explain to them why. Another way is to let them think and decide for themselves. This way, you give your

CH#2 - Motivation

players autonomy, and you tap into their intrinsic motivation. Asking questions is a good tool to do so.

When you have the ball at your feet, you can do many things. But basically, it boils down to one of these three things: you dribble, you pass the ball, or you shoot the ball towards the goal. In what situation would you choose to dribble?

You give the player the chance to think for and decide for himself what to do. Does the player find it too difficult to answer? Good, then you are teaching him something. In that case, give him options to choose from.

"You just started dribbling. Is it better to dribble if there is a defender in front of you, or is it better to dribble when there is no defender in front of you? And do you want to explain your answer to me?" If your player still has no idea at all, you help him by explaining how you see it. With your explanation, you give him a chance to understand. "If a defender stands in front of you and puts pressure on you, there will be space somewhere else on the pitch. Then it is often better to pass the ball to a teammate with more space. When the defender is moving backwards and shields your teammate, there is no pressure on you. Then there is space on the field around you. Then you can best use that space for dribbling." Kobe Bryant also liked to ask his players questions. Bryant was a five-time basketball champion in the NBA and coach of his daughter's basketball team. In an interview, he was asked about his experience standing aside the pitch. "Great fun," he replied. "Because I get the chance to watch and ask questions, I see asking questions as my task as a coach. We would probably win more if I "micromanage" during the game, if I told them what to do. But we watch and let the players discover and experience themselves. Because we think of the long term and want the players to be the best basketball players they can be," he continued to inform.

Watch the entire interview with the link "Chapter 2.2 Kobe Bryant" at https://www.bauer-vandelooij.nl/bijlage-boek.

Being able to choose and decide for yourself often provides pleasure – intrinsic motivation.

You can offer your players choices in how to play a match. For example, in which position does someone want to play? I always listen to a player who wants to play in a certain position. That's not to say that I do put him in his favorite position because he wants to. But if he comes up with arguments that convince me, then I give him his chance. He's the one playing, after all. You can also offer choices for your team. How do you want to press the opponent? How do you want to build up? What is the goal for this season? The team has to do it on the pitch. Of course, you have much more overview, and you can come up with a good plan, but why wouldn't you want your players to come up with a plan themselves? They think about it carefully and experience whether the plan works by executing it. When formulating their plan, you can help them by asking critical questions. Afterwards, you evaluate the plan and execution together. Another benefit of asking questions is that your players become aware of what they already know and are able to understand. Sometimes players find out they know more than they initially thought because they are making plans themselves.

- *Offer your players choices, then you respond to their need for autonomy. That makes them intrinsically more motivated. In addition, they learn to deal with responsibility, and they become independent and more creative.*

Let Your Players Judge for Themselves

Players must give 100 percent every training session to learn and perform optimally. That requires discipline. It's human to struggle with that sometimes. In those cases, they need you to put focus on. Address your players by their need for autonomy. Let your players judge and decide to give that 100 percent again.

At PSV, I led a training session where the first exercise revolved around motor skills, so that players learned to move better, faster, and more agile. Players went through a course in which they performed different forms of movement. During the first round, I felt frustration bubbling up within me. Some players executed the exercises seriously, but most of them didn't. Of course, I understand that the roof does not always come off during a training session, and sometimes, there can be a less serious training session. But not this one, besides, there were other moments to be less serious in training sessions. If you are ambitious, train ambitiously too, I think. Do your best. After the first round, I called the players together. While they came to me, I thought of what the other coaches on the field and the parents next to the pitch might think. That thought increased my frustration. The group of players was right in front of me. What would you tell them? Where I sometimes shared my frustration in similar situations, I now opted for a different strategy.

It is reassuring for players if they can be who they are. That they do not have to twist turns for a positive judgment from another but can judge themselves. Only the player himself judges whether his behavior is in line with how he wants to behave. I decided on throwing this bow. I shared my observations from the first round with the players by telling them my personal view,

"I saw most of you not completing the exercises completely, executing movements half-heartedly, and playing with each other. What I saw, raised questions. Questions such as: Do they want to train seriously? Do they want to give their best to become a better player?"

After this, I linked those observations to their purpose, "What is your goal in playing at PSV? I think you all wish to become a better player and preferably become professional. Is that right? If so, you have to train. Which way of training suits your goal best: giving 100 percent or giving less than 100 percent? "

Finally, I gave the players the space to make their own judgments, "Think for a moment about what you came here to do, what you want to achieve, and whether you're on the right track with your behavior from the first round. It doesn't really matter to me whatever you choose. It is always good because you have to do what you want. Do know that we are engaged in training good players at PSV. In our eyes, that comes with you giving everything you've got in every training session. You decide whether that suits you. In a moment, we will proceed to the second round, and then I see in your behavior whatever choice you make." Sparks flew off in the second block, and in the third too.

In every team, there's a hierarchy, and there are leaders and followers. You can use this in managing the team. You can address leaders in front of the whole group or take them apart. When your

CH#2 - Motivation

team leaders pick up on your advice, they're likely to lead the team automatically by giving the right example or coaching their teammates. Moreover, every player on the team experiences that you care about the behavior and that you give feedback to all the players, whether he's the best or worst player on the team.

Take a leader of the group aside and ask him, "What is your goal? Does your behavior help you towards your goal? What do you want on game day? Would you rather win or lose? How can you make the chance of winning as great as possible? Indeed, when you give 100 percent and improve your performance that also applies to your teammates. Do you know why I'm picking you out? You are an example for the rest of the group. You put a standard for the rest with your behavior. With that, you can stimulate your teammates. What if you are late? What if you don't give 100 percent? What influence does that have on the rest of the team do you think? And what if you arrive on time and go full throttle? How would that affect the rest of the team? Think about how you can increase the odds of winning the match. Then decide what influence you want to have on your teammates."

You can recognize the leaders in your team by their behavior and how the group responds to them. They are the players who determine, and are followed by teammates. Often times, the better players on the team are the leaders.

Who determines how a player behaves, the coach or the player?

That's an interesting question.

In another training session, we did a rondo. One of the two defenders did not give 100 percent in my opinion, which made his co-defender completely break down, to no avail. I stopped the exercise and asked the less committed defender about our way of defending, the goal, and his behavior, "How do we defend?"

The player was uncomfortable turning, but gave the answer that suited our way of playing: "Full of pressure to get the ball back as soon as possible."

"Exactly. Will you explain to me why you are not defending in that way? "I confronted him.

He raised his shoulders.

"Maybe you have a good reason?"

He didn't.

"Then I want to see in your behavior that you do everything you can to conquer that ball back as quickly as possible. That's what we expect from each other in the way we defend. That means you don't press at a walking pace, but at high speed. This increases the chance that the opponent will make a mistake. "

In my view, you determine the goals together with your players. You agree on the behavior that goes with it. You monitor these goals and behavior. Behavior has consequences, of course. If the player from the example remains to press at a walking pace, the consequence is that he will not play a lot in my team. He does not give 100 percent, but giving 100 percent is the basis for me. However, the only one who judges his behavior is the player himself, not me. The player is also the one who decides what to do with that judgment. He decides whether to change his behavior, not me or his teammates. My role is to mirror the player's behavior against the goal because maybe he is unaware of his behavior.

- *Let your players judge for themselves, then you respond to their need for autonomy. This fuels their intrinsic motivation. In addition, they learn to reflect on and judge their behavior, ideally in a relationship to their goals.*

CH#2 - Motivation

Let Your Players Try and Make Mistakes

So many things that could be improved happen on the pitch. Therefore, you could continuously tell your players what needs to be improved. You can coach them everything on everything. How would that be for your players? Do you like it if your boss gives you continuous feedback on everything you do? Probably not. Also, players do not feel the need to hear from the coach every time. They do need the freedom to try to do what they think is right.

When you come to watch a training session of mine, you might sometimes be wondering if I am present, whether I see what happens while they're playing. You will not hear me for minutes. There is a thought behind that. During my training, I often do three or four exercises. We regularly play three blocks per exercise. Before the first block, I explain the rules of the exercise, and I answer any questions players might have. If the rules are clear, the exercise begins. During the first block, I often don't say anything. That has an advantage that I can observe very well what is happening, but that is bycatch. The idea is that players get the freedom to try and make mistakes in block 1.

After block 1, I ask them about their experience, "What makes it hard to score points? How can your teammates help you? What's the effect of putting pressure on the ball immediately after you lose it?"

We draw a few conclusions by naming skills that are helpful, and we want to see more. In blocks two and three, I coach more on those skills.

Another way to give your players the time and space to try is the standard response that Remco Wortel, my assistant trainer at Willem II, and I gave to "may I" questions from our players. Players often ask for consent, even if the manner of play is clear and the appropriate behavior is concrete. These queries are usually in the form of questions such as, "May I come forward? May I change positions? May I run here?" Our standard answer to that question is, "Do what you want."

Of course, the answer is a bit more nuanced because we are not a circus. But the players know what we mean because of our explanation to previous "may I" questions with those four words.

Do what you think is right and make agreements with your teammates if needed. Doesn't it turn out to be a success afterwards? A great experience from which we help you learn.

An extreme example of behavior that follows our standard response is perhaps what happened during an exhibition game. The score was 1-1, with one or two minutes to play when we got a corner kick. In our dugout, with four or five substitutes and our team manager, the consternation was born when our goalkeeper decided to leave his goal and went for the opponent's box. In the field, other players took positions around the middle line so that the goalkeeper could go forward. But still, our goal was empty. The corner kick was taken, and the ball hit the head of our goalkeeper, who scored the winning goal 1-2. A great moment for our keeper and the rest of the team to remember. He dared to come forward because he knew our answer to the *may I* questions.

Of course, it sometimes goes wrong. In fact, it probably will more often go wrong than it succeeds when players try things, especially if they have to try something for the first time. Ruud van Nistelrooij compared learning to play soccer with learning to walk. He told me, "You let the child walk, and you, as a parent, walk behind it. You are not going to push your child over, but it will fall. That is what happens when learning to walk. If the child falls, pick it up. But you don't take the bumps or obstacles from the path. Falling is part of learning to walk. "

Learning to play soccer better means making mistakes. I'm not saying players have to go out to the pitch and consciously make as many mistakes as possible, but it does ring a bell when a player does everything right repeatedly and makes no mistakes. Is this player being challenged enough? By making mistakes, your player works on skills that he hasn't mastered yet. Moreover, mistakes can lead to more motivation for your player; what he cannot do yet, he will want to do better next time. Learning to play soccer better can be exciting because your player is getting out of his comfort zone. Within his comfort zone, a player does what he already can and knows.

For example, playing with the right foot because he is right-footed. It becomes interesting when the player steps out of his comfort zone. If that happens, your role becomes crucial because the chances of errors increase.

How do you react to your player's mistakes? With what you do, say, and radiate with his mistake, you set the tone. You, thereby, give a signal for the following situations in which the player has a choice between taking a risk and going for safety. Suppose your right-footed player goes outside his comfort zone and passes the ball with the tip of his left foot. What signal do you give him when you tell him to pass the next ball with his right foot instead of his left foot? And what signal do you give when you tell him it's better to pass the ball with the inside of his left foot the next time? In the first case, you give him the signal that you are all about results. Players should do what they already can because then the chance of making a mistake is smaller, and the chance of a result is bigger. Will your players choose safety or risk in future situations? In the second case, you give him the signal that you are all about improving performance. Players are allowed to do what they already can and try what they cannot do yet. Will your players in future situations choose safety or risk?

Of course, players may still opt for safety, even if you give them the freedom to take risks. However, the player then has at least had the choice. If you coach on results, you give the player actually no choice, no time, and no space to try. What signal do you want to give to your players? Should they opt for safety (result), or are they allowed to take risks (try to improve their performance)?

In my view, development leads to results, but results do not per se lead to development. A player is better if he can play with both feet as opposed to only the right foot. Although, only playing with the right foot leads to more good passes, actions, assists, and goals in the short term. And in the long-term, your player cannot suddenly play football with two feet; he will have to train with his left foot. If he does, he is a better player in the long run because he has more options at his disposal. This asks of you to accept in the short term, in the here and now, that a player is going to lose ball possession by using his lesser foot to practice. It's the only way to get relatively two-footed. Therefore I sometimes applaud when a player hits the ball with his lesser foot, even if the ball goes over the fence. According to my experience, ninety-nine out of a hundred boys can learn to dribble, pass and shoot better with their lesser foot. Two-footedness is trainable, although one will learn it faster than the other.

> Spanish research in swimming has shown the effect autonomy has on the degree of stress in athletes. Two types of coaches were compared. On the one hand, there was the autocratic coach. This type of coach decides everything by himself, and he does not give autonomy to athletes. On the other side was the democratic coach. This coach listens to athletes, and he gives them autonomy. The stress level of the athletes was measured by the amount of cortisol in their bodies. Cortisol is a hormone that the human body produces during stress. The higher the cortisol level, the more stress the athlete experiences. The research showed that athletes experienced more stress, the less autonomy they were given. Conversely, they experienced less stress when given more autonomy. During the training sessions with the autocratic coach, the cortisol level of the players was higher than with the democratic coach. A little stress makes an athlete alert, but too much stress hinders learning and performance.

All in all, I give my players time and space to try what they have not yet mastered. I am convinced that with proper training, they will develop their skills. The better you match with your players' autonomy, the stronger they dare to be themselves, dare to make their own choices, and go try.

Trying is one of the strongest forms of autonomy. To dare to do what you think of in your head creates intrinsic motivation. In addition, it leads to creativity, solution-oriented learning, collaboration, and improved performance.

Do you not believe that your players can decide and arrange things themselves? Then go have a look at soccer courts or in the schoolyard during breaks, the contemporary street soccer that

The Coach Makes the Difference

Cruijff was such a fan of. There, the players decide for themselves, and there is no coach who decides for them. You can give your players autonomy, the extent of which, of course, depends on the player. One can handle more autonomy than the other, and you make that call.

• Besides the fact that autonomy increases your players' intrinsic motivation, autonomy also improves the chances your players learn to deal with freedom responsibly and creatively and learn to work together and become solution-oriented and independent.

> Google brought giving autonomy to its employees into practice with 'twenty percent time'. This means the employee could spend twenty percent of his working time on whatever he wanted. Half of Google's innovative ideas, such as Gmail, Orkut, and Google News, arose during that twenty percent time. Have you ever considered letting your players decide what to train every so often?

Table 1: Ideas for giving autonomy		
	Player decides	Coach decides
Player shows up at practice.	X	
The way a player conducts himself. Player and coach agree on desired behavior and hold each other accountable. The player, however, decides how he behaves.	X	
Team agreements. Involve players in coming to terms as a team. Decide, for example, how to respond to a mistake.	X	X
Practices during training sessions. You can involve players in what skills or tactical ideas to train on.	(X)	X

Forming teams during training sessions. Have players make teams. Prevent the classic way of choosing in which the same player is being chosen last by appointing a captain per team and having them discuss the teams together.	(X)	X
Captain during a match. You can let your players decide who's going to captain them by saying, 'Who's coaching others, helping others, and leading by example?'	(X)	X
Line up for a match. You can involve players in the lineup by saying, 'Up front, we need speed. Who's the right player for that job?'	(X)	X
Match number. You can have players choose who gets to wear which number during the match.	X	X

Training goals. You can involve a player in what he wants to learn from a training session. 'What skill do you specifically want to train?'	(X)	X
Choices during play. Have the player decide what choices to make while playing. Don't become a *PlayStation coach*, but just let him play.	X	
(X) = players decide if necessary		

The Coach Makes the Difference

Summary

What can you, as a coach, do to motivate your players intrinsically through autonomy?

Offer them choices

Let your players judge for themselves

Let your players try and make mistakes

2.3 Competence

- Do You Look At What Your Players Can Do?

    "I've never done it before, so I think I can do it."

    -Pippi Longstocking

What answer do your players give when you ask them what they prefer to do? Chances are they will name something they are good at. You, me, your players, everyone likes to do what they do well. It feels good when things work out. It satisfies the need for competence. You feel competent when things work out, and others see it. It is much more fun to fix a tire if you actually succeed in doing so. It is much more fun to speak Spanish when you find that Spaniards can understand what you say. It's a lot more fun to keep the ball high if you can. And it's great when others confirm and acknowledge that you can do something well.

Doing what you can do well makes you feel that what you do is useful and that you contribute to something. The need for competence is the second factor leading to intrinsic motivation. Already it has been shown that competence only improves intrinsic motivation when someone feels he himself is responsible for the successful behavior. Competence must always be accompanied by a sense of autonomy. What can you, the coach, do to increase the sense of competence in your players? Focus on what your player can do, offer an appropriate challenge, and value effort and initiative.

Focus On What Your Player Can Do

Alex van Roessel, goalkeeper coach at the Willem II Soccer Academy, told me a nice anecdote about parents in today's society,

The Coach Makes the Difference

"A child comes home with his school report card in his pocket. He's got one nine, three eights, two sevens, three sixes, a five, and a four. What do parents start talking about? About the four and the five. Many parents look at what a child cannot do and what is not there. The same trend is common in soccer. What do we achieve with that?"Coaches look at what players cannot do and coach them accordingly. That is an essential part of coaching; you help your players do things they could not do at that level before, with the effect of players knowing how they can improve themselves. But, an approach focusing on everything that players cannot do, on what isn't there yet, can have detrimental effects. It can cause you to become negative towards your players, which can eventually lead to a sense of *No matter what I do, it is never good*. Many youth players of various levels and ages tell me they have experienced a coach with such an approach. It demotivated them to play football, and they had even thought about quitting. How many players have actually quit because of coaches that only focus on what is not going well, on what is not there? Fortunately, you can also choose a different approach.

It is Saturday morning, and my team is participating in a two-day tournament. Our first group match is in an hour and a half. Tournaments are a wonderful experience for players, especially when they are as young as my players were, about ten years old. In the preliminary discussion of the upcoming two days, I had the name of every player written on the coaching board. I told them they knew how we wanted to play and what kind of memory we wanted to give the audience. After all, we had trained for almost a season and already discussed what was important to us as a team. The most important thing, for now, was the coaching board.

Boys, you all know Arjen Robben, right?"

Yes, they all knew him.

"What is Robben's weapon?"

Soon they came up with the answer that Robben, as a right winger, dribbles from the right to the center so that he gets the ball in front of his left foot, which often leads to a chance or goal.

"Exactly, and I think everyone knows Robben goes from the outside to inside. His opponents are preparing for this. Their coaches probably even tell them Robben is going to do that. Despite the defenders being prepared for it, Robben succeeds almost every time. He dribbles past his opponent by coming in, and then he scores with his left foot. He has scored many goals like that. Why is that?'

This is a more difficult and broad question for this age, yet one answers, "Because he's super good at it."

"Exactly! Robben is so good that he succeeds almost every time, even though everyone knows what he's going to do. How's his right foot? How's his defending? Is he good at heading the ball? No, those are not his qualities, really. Robben is not good at everything. But he is super good at going inside. He has become so good that he has been playing at the highest level for years. We can learn something from that. Here you see your names on the coach-board. In a moment, you can write what you think you are really good at as a player. You write down your weapon. The goal of this tournament is that you, in the matches you play, show and practice your weapon as much as possible."

With this goal, I put the focus on what my players felt they were good at. I didn't look at what they couldn't do yet, but I looked at what they could and wanted to do. A nice alternative is to let players tell each other the strengths they see in one another.

Another way to focus on what players can do is by sometimes giving players the role of coach. During the season, I repeat exercises. Plenty of players understand the exercise and therefore know what the goal is. Sometimes an exercise is not clear to others because they are from another team but are training with us, because they are on trial, or because they simply have forgotten. When players know the goal of the exercise, I hand them the opportunity to explain the exercise to the other players. Are they always complete and clear in their explanation? Certainly not, but then others or myself can add.

Okay, player X has already told two of the three rules. Who can add the last rule?

We tie in with what the player has already told us. Not from what he hasn't. Otherwise, my response would be, *Okay, player X didn't recall and explain it fully. Which rule is he missing?*

The difference may be paper thin, but I am convinced that that small difference can have a big impact.

• *Looking at what a player can do leads to a sense of competence. That increases his intrinsic motivation and self-confidence and the chance that he will play with more guts.*

Offer Your Players an Appropriate Challenge

Your players feel competent when they do things successfully. And especially if they do something they couldn't do before. By passing a ball with the right foot to a teammate whilst being left-footed, a player can play well as a right-winger instead of a right-back too, and he can also play well when he is playing with another team. To increase the feeling of competence, it is important that what the player does, matches his qualities. A player of fourteen will generally feel a low level of competence when playing against players of eighteen. A U17 team generally does not feel very competent in a match against a first team. A pupil at primary school generally feels not as competent when he takes a math test at college level.

Conversely, an overly simple challenge does not contribute to a sense of competence. Studies have shown that high expectations set the bar high for your players and stimulate their performance and development. It is important that you also support your players in this process. You do what you can; you listen to them and give them tips, such as, to help them reach that bar.

- *The challenge you offer has to match the current level of your players. If the challenge is too easy, it will lead to boredom; if the challenge is too difficult, then stress or panic arises.*

The challenge you offer is one of the most important resources you have, to help your players develop. In my experience, varying levels are great. Sometimes the challenge is easy, sometimes difficult, and sometimes the challenge is around your players 'level. Ideally, the challenge is just above their current level, so the player must give a hundred percent to improve his performance. A good measure to match the challenge to your players 'level exists. You can use this measure anytime, anywhere. No matter who your players are, regardless of their level or preferred foot, you can use this measure. This measure is the level of the player himself. A player can always be compared to himself. By doing so, he learns whether his football achievements are improving or not.

I divided the team into three groups. They do the same exercise and are given the same amount of time to perform that exercise. Each group plays three rounds at the same time. In each round, the previous score is the measure for the next round. The goal is to improve as a group per round. Did group A just get eight points? In the next round, they go for a minimum of nine points. Did group B just score twelve points? In the next round, they go for at least thirteen points. In this way, you don't compare between groups, you compare a group with their previous performance, and you compare them with themselves. Thus, the challenge suits every group of players, and they will, despite the differences in performance between the groups, feel competent.

During training sessions, you often have the reins; that's where you determine the challenge. How do you do that in the league? You have been assigned to a league and the teams in that league, and you have to do it with them. What do you do when the opponents are much better or too low-level? How can you still match the challenge to the level of your players?

You can contact the FA (Football Association) and opt for a different league, but that does not always work. Another possibility you may have is playing practice games. A practice match is ideal because you decide which team to invite. Do you choose a team from the third division, first division, or premier division? I often watched the league opponents on Saturday and, based on that, the level of the opponent in the exhibition game. If my team had a hard time in the league, then I would schedule a practice match with an opponent that I rated lower level than my team. When it was easy in the league, I scheduled an opponent whose level I estimated to be higher than my team's. But what do you do during the league and cup matches when the differences are very big?

CH#2 - Motivation

It must have been a strange picture that Saturday morning when the referee blew the final whistle. We just lost to another team with big numbers, but I was applauding my players. We played a league game against a team that's top-level in the Netherlands. Our players were good, but not yet at the level of this opponent. We knew that beforehand, as staff. On the way to that match, we played an away game, I was thinking. We are going to play against a team that is much better than us.

How can I give the guys a suitable challenge so that they can still feel competent afterwards? In the pre-match team talk, I, therefore, gave them a challenge that, in my eyes, was feasible.

"Boys, what's very important to us in how we play? "

The answers quickly followed, "We want to seek a solution in the build-up, we help each other in the field, and we always give a hundred percent."

"Exactly, we want to show that in every match. And that can be tricky when the going gets tough in the game. You miss an opportunity, you make a mistake, or you concede a goal. That sucks, we understand that. In this match, you will miss opportunities, make mistakes and concede goals, which requires you to persevere, especially when the going gets tough. In those moments, we want to see that you continue to play according to our philosophy, continue to work together and keep giving everything.

For example, keep putting pressure as we trained. If you do all that, I am sure you will give good passes, you will complete successful dribbles, and you are going to recover balls and score goals. With the staff, we are only going to observe whether you persevere today. If you play the entire sixty minutes as we trained, give it your all, and keep working together, then we are proud."

Did my players win the match because of this? No. Was that realistic at all? No, I don't think so. The challenge I gave them was clear and more appropriate than the level of the opposing team. After every goal we conceded, and there were a lot of them, the players kept behaving like we had challenged them beforehand. They kept putting pressure, helping each other, and scoring a number of goals. I find that valuable, and I showed my players so.

Conversely, it may be that on Saturday, you will meet an opposing team that is a lot less good than your team. How, then, do you ensure a suitable challenge? In New Zealand, they have a great concept in youth rugby. They aim to have every match end tight, preferably a draw. If they notice that one team is much better than the other team, they mix the two teams so that the level of both teams is roughly the same. Then every player has to work hard, and the challenge fits the level of most players better. I've experienced some Dutch coaches who do appreciate this concept, but most of them don't yet. We are not that far yet. What does work, is coming up with goals that challenge your players.

A great challenge, in my eyes, which also helps players develop more broadly, is to rotate positions. In the 6v6, 8v8, or even the 11v11 matches, your players switch positions after every goal or every so many minutes. That creates chaos, and your players have to deal with it. This makes the match more equal. Another benefit is that your players experience what it is like to be in a position that is new to them. They, for example, learn to unmark in a different way or defend in another way. Will your striker be a center-back? There he experiences what it is like for a defender, in both offensive and defensive terms. In possession, he dribbles and notices that his fellow players up front can help him by un-marking. Vice versa, he learns what an opposing striker does that makes defending difficult. These are lessons he can use to his advantage when playing up front again.

Another challenge that I have used is playing soccer with your lesser foot. There are plenty of options you have to make the challenge better match the level of your players. With some challenges, you have to be careful, and you don't want to embarrass the opponents and their coach. For some reason, many coaches and clubs like to play in the strongest league with their team. Of course, that is nice for your ego, but does it also fit with the level of your players? In my view, playing in the strongest league doesn't have to be a goal. Each team can best play at the level that suits the level of the players in the team. How much fun is playing at the highest level if you lose every game without a chance? A season is very long, plus there is a risk your players will lose their competent feeling. It is also of no use for your team to become champion with both hands tied behind the back. Even then, a season lasts long. Where's the challenge? What will your players learn that season? That's why I don't think it's a disaster if you and your team are not participating at the top level. That's why I also don't think it's a disaster if your team doesn't become champions. Play at the level that suits your players 'qualities. That's best if you appreciate long-term development in youth soccer.

• Providing the right challenge is one of the strongest forms of competence. Having to do your very best with the chance of success ensures intrinsic motivation. In addition, you learn how to deal with ups and downs and tension, and it increases resilience.

Value Effort And Initiative

How nice is it when your boss or manager tells you that he appreciates you for your time and effort in doing your work? Of course, you know that you are doing your best, but it is nice when someone else notices that and confirms you. That feeds your need for competence. That is how it works for your players too. They do their best on the pitch and do a lot of things well. They probably know this, but also, for them, it is nice if you, the coach, see that and reassure their feelings.

Showing effort and taking the initiative are two behaviors that lead to a chance of success, whatever your definition of success is. In fact, effort and initiative are necessary because, without that, nothing will happen. If your players do not take the initiative to come to the training session, you can cancel it. When your central defender has the ball, but the midfielders are not making an effort to get free from their opponent, it becomes difficult to play soccer for your team.

Yet showing effort and initiative are often taken for granted. Isn't it normal for every player to do that? Perhaps it is. But what is the effect if you explicitly value them for it? We had a player who was great at dribbling. That was his weapon, and he was one of the best dribblers I've seen in all these years. He only had one problem, if he got into a 1v1 situation, nothing happened. He preferred to play the ball safely back to his teammates. We tried anything to make him dribble and use his weapon. We named his weapon, gave him tips for the 1v1, practiced body feints, and told him it didn't matter if he lost the ball, but nothing helped.

How do you stimulate a player who is so great at dribbling but doesn't dare to do so? We were at our wits 'end. Until we found the solution. We set a goal about effort and initiative and coached him accordingly. The goal was that he had to take action if he got the chance. We agreed we would keep track of the times he went for a dribble if he got into a promising situation. We gave him those statistics as feedback. We also discussed which situations were deemed promising. A 1v3 situation is not the most promising, but a 1v1 with space behind his opponent, for example, is. We agreed not to look at the success of his dribbles, and it didn't matter. As if from scratch, this player started to do what he was good at again, dribbling. It is the same player who trains with the same players on the same training field with the same coaches. But because we adjusted his goal and our coaching, the player changed his behavior.

During our feedback, we appreciated his effort and initiative, "It's great that you dribbled in seven of the nine possible situations today!"

That gave him a sense of competence which fueled his courage to dribble the next time. And the bycatch? He learned to recognize situations where dribbling was possible. That helped him go past his opponent without our focus being on that result. This is a special example of the power of appreciation for effort and initiative. Even without a specific problem or challenge, can you show your appreciation for effort and initiative? Do you see your player doing his best or taking the initiative? Name it and compliment him. The player thus learns that effort and initiative become appreciated and will show that behavior more often, with the logical consequence that the chance of successful performance increases.

- *The great thing about showing effort and taking the initiative is your players have complete control over those behaviors. Each player decides the degree of effort and initiative, whatever the situation. How big or small the opponents are, no matter how hot or cold it is, how good or bad the night's sleep was, you always determine whether you are full throttle or not. You decide whether you take the initiative or not. When your goal is to take the initiative, you will almost always feel competent.*

Factors Undermining Effort and Initiative

Playing successfully does not always give a player the feeling of competence, unfortunately. Maybe the opponent was too young or not at the level. Players, no matter how young or old, are really aware of this. Are your players happier when they compete in a tough match with an exciting 3-2 win or when they win 10-0 freewheeling against the opponent? Again, the challenge is important.

In addition, your role in their success is a determining factor for their sense of competence because was your player himself responsible for his success, or did he just follow your instructions? The latter has a negative effect on competence. Instructing players what to do whilst standing at the sideline can be dangerous and is a pitfall for many. Players who constantly follow explicit instructions from the coach or parents often do not develop a stronger sense of competence. Only when your players experience that their own choices lead to success, will their sense of competence grow.

- *If you or their parents tell a player what he should do, it may increase the chances of short-term success, but the long-term effects are not that great. Not for his intrinsic motivation nor for learning to play football.*

CH#2 - Motivation

If you continuously instruct your players what to do, they become dependent on you. As a result, they generally do not learn to play football better; they learn to follow instructions. They learn to obey. What happens if you're not there? Or, suppose you have a player who likes to make his own choices. What should he do if his choice differs from your instruction? Should he listen to you or himself?

These are some of the risks of continuous instructions on the sideline:

Your players no longer take the initiative, do not come up with any ideas or solutions in football situations themselves, and do not develop creativity – In short, next to reduced intrinsic motivation, you hardly develop your players to be independent and creative.

I have experienced for myself how difficult it can be not to tell players what to do. During a training exercise or a match, you see your players having a hard time. They struggle to recognize the opponent's patterns and aren't able to find the solution, or you see that the opponent is playing better or is even winning, which all make it difficult. You want to get the most out of every training session and match, both in terms of performance improvement of the individual or team as well as the match result. Then there's the opinion others hold about you as a coach. You want to look good with people within the club, with parents, with the public, or perhaps even with the press. What they think of you is important to you, and that is human. All these factors together make it very tempting to tell players what to do so you raise the chances of short-term success. That is not surprising, but now you know the risks of it in the long run. What you choose, short or long-term, is up to you. That has to do with what you stand for as a coach.

The Coach Makes the Difference

- *Appreciating effort and initiative from your players increases their feeling of competence. Give your players the opportunity to make their own choices on the pitch. This not only leads to more intrinsic motivation for your players but also to creativity, independence, and more effort and initiative in the future.*

CH#2 - Motivation

Summary

What can you, as a coach, do to motivate a player more intrinsically through competence?

Focus on what your player can do

Offer your players an appropriate challenge

Value effort and initiative

2.4 RELATEDNESS

- Does Everyone Belong?

"Our need to belong is not rational, but it is a constant that exists across all people in all cultures."

- Simon Sinek

Three friends play with a ball. They throw the ball at each other until its pattern is broken. Apparently, two of the three friends found a new game. A game for two. They just throw the ball between the two of them. It's a new pattern. The third is standing there and looking at it.

Relatedness is the third component of intrinsic motivation and means that you belong and other people care about you. Being connected with others is not just another buzzword or hype. You are genetically and evolutionary programmed to be connected with others, it is good and healthy for your brain.

You see relatedness in a team when every player is involved by others, and no one is left out. The ultimate state of connection ensures players feel so good within the team that they can deliver their maximum performance. Connecting is hearing, seeing, and acknowledging the other. A connection exists already between two people, between you and your player. Without a relationship, there is no performance. How do you establish a connection? Accept the player, create a 'we-feeling, 'and show interest in the person.

Accept The Player

Most players feel best when they can behave in a way that suits them. They have their qualities, their whims, and their imperfections, and they can all be. Your recognition and acceptance that every player is different, helps your players feel best. It enables them to perform and develop optimally. You can show your players that the differences between them are not scary or dangerous. Those differences connect them.

I looked for that connection during a tournament at the start of the season.

"Boys, we are all different. Those differences can sometimes be felt as if one is worth more than the other. There are people who believe differences are scary. But I believe that differences can actually make us stronger. A stronger team."

Then I ask my goalkeeper, "What are you good at?"

"Goalkeeping!"

"What position in the field do you want to be in?"

"In the goal."

"That's great. Do you know why?"

The players look at me.

I address our striker, "What are you good at?"

"Scoring goals."

"Where would you prefer to be on the field?"

"In the front, close to the opponent's goal."

"I thought so! You should be happy that our goalkeeper is in our goal because then you don't have to stand there. That does not suit your qualities because they lie in scoring goals. If we put you in the goal, you probably have less fun playing football. In the other way around, our goalkeeper is happy with you! Otherwise, he could not stand in our goal, and he had to be in the front. But his qualities lie precisely in preventing opponents from scoring. So we are all different; we look different, we maybe think different, and we may have different preferences and qualities, and that's great! We complement each other with our unique qualities. That makes us a stronger team."

Differences connect because they strengthen players and teams. Differences also exist between you and your players. Your players can come up with very creative answers to questions, situations, or problems. Sometimes they have a completely different view of a situation. That is shifting gears. At the same time, that's great because the player indicates what he thinks. And because it is different from what you had conceived or expected, you can talk to each other.

"Why do I find x, and why do you think y?" It takes both of you further, for it makes you look in a different way. Moreover, you hear, see, and acknowledge the player. You accept him and his vision. How good, bad, rightly or wrongly that is. That view gives you insight into this player and may offer you the opportunity to connect better with him. That's also one of the tips psychologist Daniel Goleman has for leaders: listen to your team members. Hear them out about their ambitions, ideas and plans. It will serve you better both.

- *Recognizing and accepting the player and his input creates a connection. It offers players the chance to be themselves and increase their performance on the pitch. In addition, players who see and experience these mutual differences are okay and can strengthen the team.*

Create A We-Feeling

If you have a common goal, a team goal, individual differences can strengthen each other. In fact, you need them. One of the holy grails in a team sport is for the individual player to subordinate his own interests to contribute to the team's interest. The player can rely on fellow players and his fellow players on him. A player feels that teammates would do the same for him as what he does for them, for the team. How do you turn a group of players into one team? There are many ways.

The most important thing you can do, as a coach, is to involve every player on the team and not exclude or ignore anyone. Is a player, for example, injured? Show interest in him and give him a role to help the team. For example, make him an assistant coach. Is a player on the bench? Involve him with the team by letting him watch what the opponent does so that he can share his findings and give advice to his team during halftime.

Another important tool you can use is to set a common goal. What do we want to achieve as a team? How do we want to behave as a team? Agree on this as a team and monitor this with your players. Or let your players monitor the agreements. Set them free and give them the responsibility to lead. Develop leaders by giving those players what embodies the team goal and behavior. They are the example and oversee the we-feeling. Various studies have shown the impact of these leaders on the team and we-feeling.

Another way to increase the connection within your team is to emphasize exclusivity, how special it is that members are part of the team. You create that exclusivity by setting the bar. The higher the bar, the more difficult it is to join this team. Being on this team becomes valuable. The best-known bar to being part of a soccer team is the soccer level of the players. In my opinion, not the best bar to create a connection. Within our team, we wanted a bar over which our players had more control. Because anyone would want to be at the level of Messi, but how many succeed?

Our bar concerns the behavior of the players and of the staff because you can always fully control behavior yourself, barring exceptions. A bar focused on behavior connects players and staff because if you do you the same you feel one. During a tournament at the start of this season, we players and staff, jointly set that bar.

The staff asked the players various questions like, "What is success? What impression do we want to make on others? How do we want to appear as a team? What can a teammate do to damage your trust? What can a teammate do to earn your trust?" Every player and every staff member was given the space to have his say. As a result, we created a clear and concrete bar with team agreements. One of those team agreements was *a promise is a promise*. To us, that was a sign of trust in each other. And we found trust to be the basis of connection. If we agree to train, we have to be there. If we agree that the goalkeeper is in the goal, he does not take on the role of attacker. If he does, then it becomes difficult for his fellow players and us, the staff, to trust him.

A concrete standard within, '*a promise is a promise*' was that every player would be on time at the training field. That is to say, before the start of the training session. If a player was late, he did not train and did not play on Saturday. So there was something at stake because every player on this team wanted to train and play on Saturday. My players came to the club with vans that picked them up from school. If these vans were late, then still, the players arrived on time for practice. The players invented creative solutions to save time. It was great to see. Was no player late for a training session? Fortunately, there were some at the beginning of the season. Fortunately? Yes, because those are opportunities for you as a coach to show whether the agreements you have made are hard or not. Then players get to know you and the staff.

CH#2 - Motivation

Those few moments do something with you, of course. One boy was thirty seconds late. While the tears were rolling down his cheeks, I sent him back to the locker room, "Go do your school homework."

On one of those occasions, two players were late because the van was late. However, they were in the same van as some of the others players who were on time. In that situation, we chose to let the team decide because we were curious to what extent the players were capable of guarding the bar. In addition, the two players that were late were among the better players on the team. What would the team decide? It was wonderful to see how they consulted with each other and how fast they made the decision.

"A promise is a promise, I think."

"But that's sad for them."

"Yes, but aren't we a team? Can we not help them?"

"Last time, there were also players late. They were also not allowed to train."

"Yes, but if we let them participate now, they can help us if we have at times to be late."

"That may be, but what is '*a promise is a promise*' worth? We don't agree on this for nothing, right?"

"Exactly, it is tough for them, but when you are late, you will not train. That is the appointment."

"'*A promise is a promise*' applies to everyone. That's why we are one team."

In about two minutes, eighteen twelve-year-olds had given each other space to have their say, and together they decided to hold these two teammates to the agreement. Too late is no training. The team guarded the bar. At that moment, I felt two emotions. On the one side, I felt sad for those two players, and this emotion will always be. You never get used to seeing someone, especially a child, in pain. On the other hand, I felt proud. The team showed itself to be a team. The players consulted with each other, but they kept the bar high. Do you want to join the team? Fine, but that involves certain agreements. And certain behavior. Where our bar was, was clear to everyone, and that characterizes a team. How many players do you think have arrived too late after this?

I can imagine that you are wondering to what extent this is justified. Is this not just the age-old punishment? Not in my opinion. To me, these are consequences of behavior.

Here are some examples of my view, a passenger arriving late at the gate misses his plane. Is that a punishment the pilot or flight attendant imposes, or is it a consequence of being late? If you don't eat, you will eventually get a stomach ache. Is that a punishment that your body imposes on you, or is it a consequence of not eating? In football, I think it works the same way. During the match, it can happen that our defender passes the ball into the feet of the opponent's striker. Of course, he doesn't do that on purpose, he wants to keep the ball in the team, but it still goes wrong. After losing the ball, the defender does everything he can to keep the striker from scoring. But the striker goes for our goal to score, of course. If he succeeds, we concede a goal, unfortunately. Isn't this fair, then? Is it a punishment?

If so, should my defender, I, or anyone else on our team ask the referee or opposing coach to replay the situation? Because otherwise, my defender takes it as a punishment? Of course not. Conceding a goal is the consequence of behavior. If we lose the ball to the opponent, we give them a chance to score. So? With your behavior, make sure you keep the ball in the team.

If you rethink, you can see the consequence as something positive. Our defender either learns to pass the ball faster, use a different timing, or has to look closer before passing the ball. The player that arrives late, learns to perhaps change clothes before checking his phone in the future. Fooling around is allowed, and there's enough time for that after we have performed. Consequences are lessons for your players.

- *I think it is my job, as a coach, to develop the players in my team and train and educate them. Pain, misfortune, sadness, and setbacks are part of the deal, just like fun, joy, or pride.*

Finally, every player is free to join the team or not. The player decides whether the team's bar suits him. He decides which team he wants to belong to. During the season, two of my players decided to quit the team because our bar and environment at that time did not suit them. Great, they found out and had the courage to admit it. Because in the end, it's all about players feeling good in order to have as much fun as possible and learn as much as possible. Don't fit in with one team? Then you look for another team.

- *No matter at what level your team plays, how well or how bad your players are, by setting a bar and making team agreements to guard that bar, you give your players a framework within which they can move. That provides clarity and creates a we-feeling that connects the team. Moreover, players learn skills they can apply anywhere in their lives. Acting towards your goal, arriving on time, or having your things in order, are appreciated in more places than just the soccer field.*

Show interest in the person

'There's no performance without a relationship 'is a frequently heard statement. Given my experiences, I agree. You can work together if you have a relationship with each other. The most important factor for this is trust. Your player trusts that you want the best for him. Do what you say and say what you actually do, that is how you prove that you're trustworthy. Conversely, you also want to trust the player. How to get that trust, and how do you build a relationship with your players?

I am a fan of Louis van Gaal's Total Person Principle. In brief, this principle implies that you not only see the player, but also the person behind the player. Of course, your player is a soccer player but he is more than that. Maybe he also has the role of son, brother, student, friend, you name it. Show interest in him as a person and in his other roles. Don't just get to know him as a player, but be sincerely interested in what's on his mind, what hobbies he has, which school subjects he likes, how things are going at home, and just whatever he wants to talk about with you. There are coaches who made an agreement with themselves to only talk about soccer-related matters on the pitch. Off the pitch, they talk about everything but soccer. I also know coaches who, prior to the season, send a questionnaire with personal questions to their players. Then they go with each player individually for at least an hour, talking about the person behind the player. Players 'reactions to this initiative are extremely positive. If you have the time, you too can get a glimpse into the life of your player by visiting him at home or at school. Not only the player thinks that it is great, but also his parents and any brothers and sisters like it.

What also helps in building a bond is that you see your player. What players like, especially the younger players, are nicknames.

A nickname gives your player the feeling that you see, appreciate, and know him. So I have given nicknames to players, and together with players, we gave coaches a nickname. The nickname I got is obvious, Maurinho. In addition to using nicknames, you can see the player in another very accessible way. Before training, you greet each player, and you get a feeling of how he is doing. You may also have a chat with him about what he experienced that day. That makes your bond broader and deeper than just being connected by soccer affairs.

That's how a player came to me with some sad news. Something happened in his life that he was dealing with, and that could have affected him on the pitch. We wanted to share that with the team.

"How awful, boy. All the best. We are there for you when you need it. What do you want in terms of the team with this? Do you want to share this with the group? And how do you want to share that?"

He indicated that he wanted to share the news, but he was unable to share it himself, so he asked if I wanted to do that. Before training, I called the group together.

"Guys, I have some sad news. One of your teammates is having a tough time, and in consultation with him, we have decided that I will tell you. Maybe some of you already know, or you have noticed something in his behavior. Unfortunately, his grandmother passed away this week."

I saw that this message had an impact on the group. The death of one's grandma or grandpa has a lot of influence on everyone, but certainly on twelve-year-olds. The boy began to cry, and my assistant coach got watery eyes too. Then as I continued talking, I noticed that my voice skipped a little.

"Can you imagine how he feels now?"

Several players nodded. Another player shared how much grief he had when his grandmother died.

"So it may be that this boy is occasionally not here with his mind. You now know why. "

As I mentioned this, the group gathered around the player, whose tears were now running down his cheeks, to wish him strength and to give him a hug. I still get goosebumps thinking back to that moment. To me, this is an example of seeing the person behind the player and how that can ensure connection within a team.

Written in the book *Pep Guardiola - Another Way to Win* by Guillem Balague, it becomes clear that Guardiola searches for and forges a strong connection with his players.

"I require the players to think collectively, otherwise, you can cannot win. You create that common feeling in the same way as what everyone desires, love. I try to manage a group of players where the person behind the player is most important."

Jürgen Klopp goes one step further in his book *Bring the Noise*, "A coach who doesn't feel love for his players cannot be a good coach."

Seattle Seahawks 'coach Peter Carrol and sports psychologist Dr. Michael Gervais swear by their connection with their players. In their culture, relationships are central. The dot on the horizon for them is love for and genuinely caring about the people they work with.

"Because in working with people, no exact formula for how to do things exists. The intention that you want the best for someone else, however, ensures that you ultimately find what works for each player. Getting close to a player is, therefore, a process," they say.

Also Sarina Wiegman, head coach of The English Lionesses, says the way to the hearts of your players is by getting connected with them. How to do that? By sharing stories about yourself with each other and by listening to your players.

I have experienced that building a good relationship with your players can be quite a challenge and can take a lot of time and patience. In my early days at PSV, I had the same team for two years. With one player, it was difficult for me to connect with. He did not trust others very fast, including me. Oftentimes, I said A, but he understood and did B. In addition, this player sometimes had a rage on the field, leaving fellow players, opponents, and parents perplexed. Since he wasn't necessarily one of the best players on the team, the question arose among some whether he should continue to play at PSV. Because I was new to PSV, a psychologist moreover, I naturally felt an extra urge to prove myself. I didn't want to let him go until I had done everything I could because I believed I could help him. Above all else, I believed this player could develop. Still, I often found myself at home being at my wits' end, what should I do with him? Fortunately, within PSV, I was able to contact Bastiaan Riemersma, coordinator, among others from PSV Academy, and Marcel van Herpen, a pedagogue. Their tips gave me new courage to help this player. I was empathetic, gave him my full attention, gave him responsibility, and set limits. I rewarded and punished him and went to visit his house and at school. In short, I tried everything to get a connection with him. Nothing seemed to work, and we still had our struggles. With time these diminished, but he remained one striking appearance and not always in the best sense of the word. When I left the team after two years, it turned out what the result was of all my frantic efforts to help him. He was quite sad about me leaving the team. Despite the struggles, a relationship of trust had arisen between us. I am still grateful to have had him on the team for two years because he didn't make it easy for me, and therefore I learned a lot about being a coach and about connecting with players.

Connection does not arise at once; every time again, you have to connect to each player. Troubles with a player don't necessarily break the connection; in fact, they can strengthen it. The connection between this player and me arose because I didn't give up. Whatever happened, I kept trying to help him. That was not the easy way. The easy way had been to let him go. Anybody would have understood that. But I wanted the best for this player. A few months after I left, I heard from our scouts that this player was doing very well, and he even stood out while playing. I was thrilled to hear that!

The person behind the player is also important at the very top level. This is evident from an episode of Tiki Taka Touzani with Wesley Sneijder. Sneijder had a successful year in 2010, he won, with his club Internazionale, the national title, the cup, the super cup, the Champions League, and the World Cup for club teams, and he played the World Cup final with the Dutch National Team. He was asked how it was possible that everything went so well in that year, and the 134-time international answered, "I felt good about myself, both soccer and private life wise. That is of course the most important thing if you feel comfortable with things at home in your private life. You have qualities, and you have a good team around you, then the rest will follow automatically."

Good well-being, with the home situation as the foundation, promotes the performance and development of your player. Does he perform less, or does he have a form dip? Then check how he is doing as a person. How are things at home? At school? You will be surprised how often underperformance on the pitch is caused by matters off the soccer pitch, like a bad report card, parents going through a divorce, or a love affair that has ended.

* *Interest in the person behind the player creates connection. It shows players that every teammate is more than alone a player, and that their coach is more than just a coach. It brings people together because they experience the same thing or share interests. In addition to intrinsic motivation, connection can lead to brotherhood, stronger cooperation on the pitch, better performance, and even friendships off the field.*

Showing or not showing interest in your players can make a difference. Simon Sinek gives an example of this in the following movie. He spoke to someone who does the same job for two different organizations. Because the managers in the two organizations are different in the way they interact with him and show interest in him in a different way, he feels and behaves in a different way too. Consequently, the way he does his work is different between the two organizations.

View the example via the link "Chapter 2.4 Simon Sinek" at https://www.bauer-vandelooij.nl/bijlage-boek.

Table 2: Don'ts and do's with regard to your players' intrinsic motivation	
DON'TS (This is how you undermine your players' intrinsic motivation)	DO'S (This is how you increase your players' intrinsic motivation)
Common ways that undermine your players' intrinsic motivation and you can best get rid of:	Common ways that play into your players' intrinsic motivation, and you better have them in your system are:
1. Reward a player for individual performance, like one euro per goal.	1. Give your players choices.
2. Continuously tell a player what he is doing and has to do.	2. Let your players judge for themselves.
3. Laugh at a player for his failed attempt to improve something.	3. Let your players try and make mistakes.
4. Assess a player continuously and continually question him.	4. Look at what your player can do.
5. Don't pay attention to a player or even ignore him.	5. Offer your players a suitable challenge.
6. Pull ahead a player or apply a double standard.	6. Appreciate effort and initiative from your players.
7. Lie to a player or don't meet your promises.	7. Accept the player.
8. Only tell a player what he cannot do or continually coach him in a negative way.	8. Create a we-feeling.
9. Shut out a player.	9. Show interest in the person behind the player.

CH#2 - Motivation

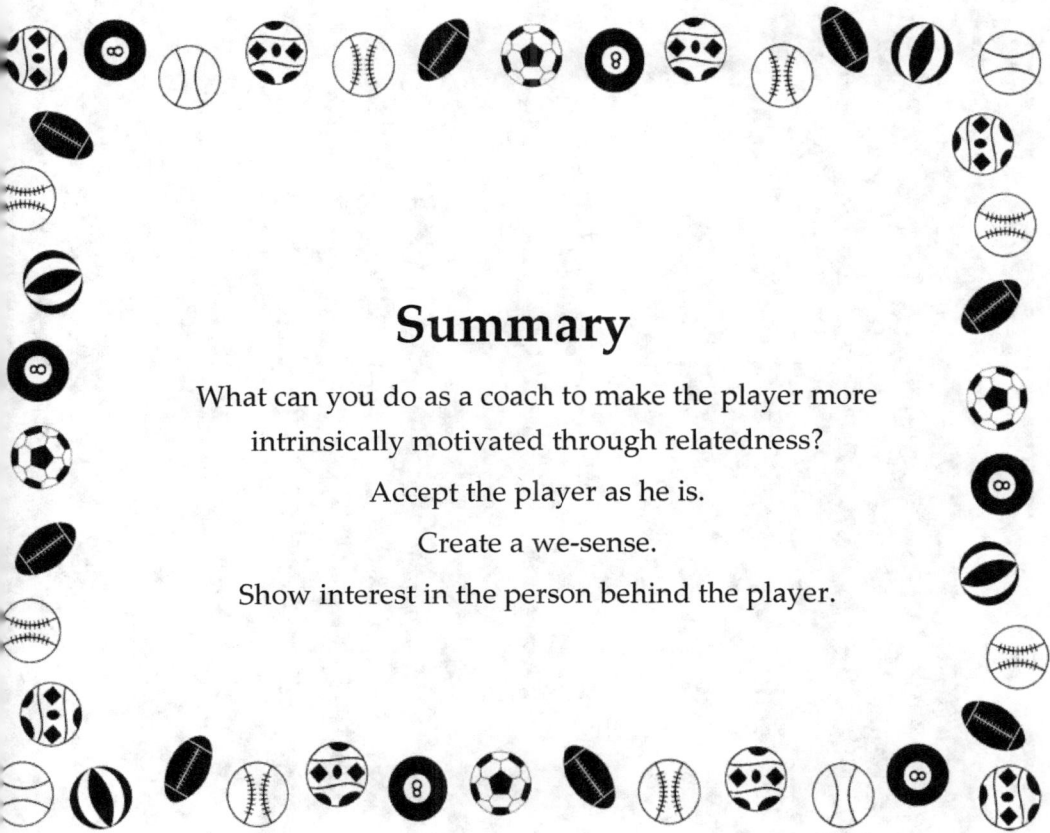

Summary

What can you do as a coach to make the player more intrinsically motivated through relatedness?

Accept the player as he is.

Create a we-sense.

Show interest in the person behind the player.

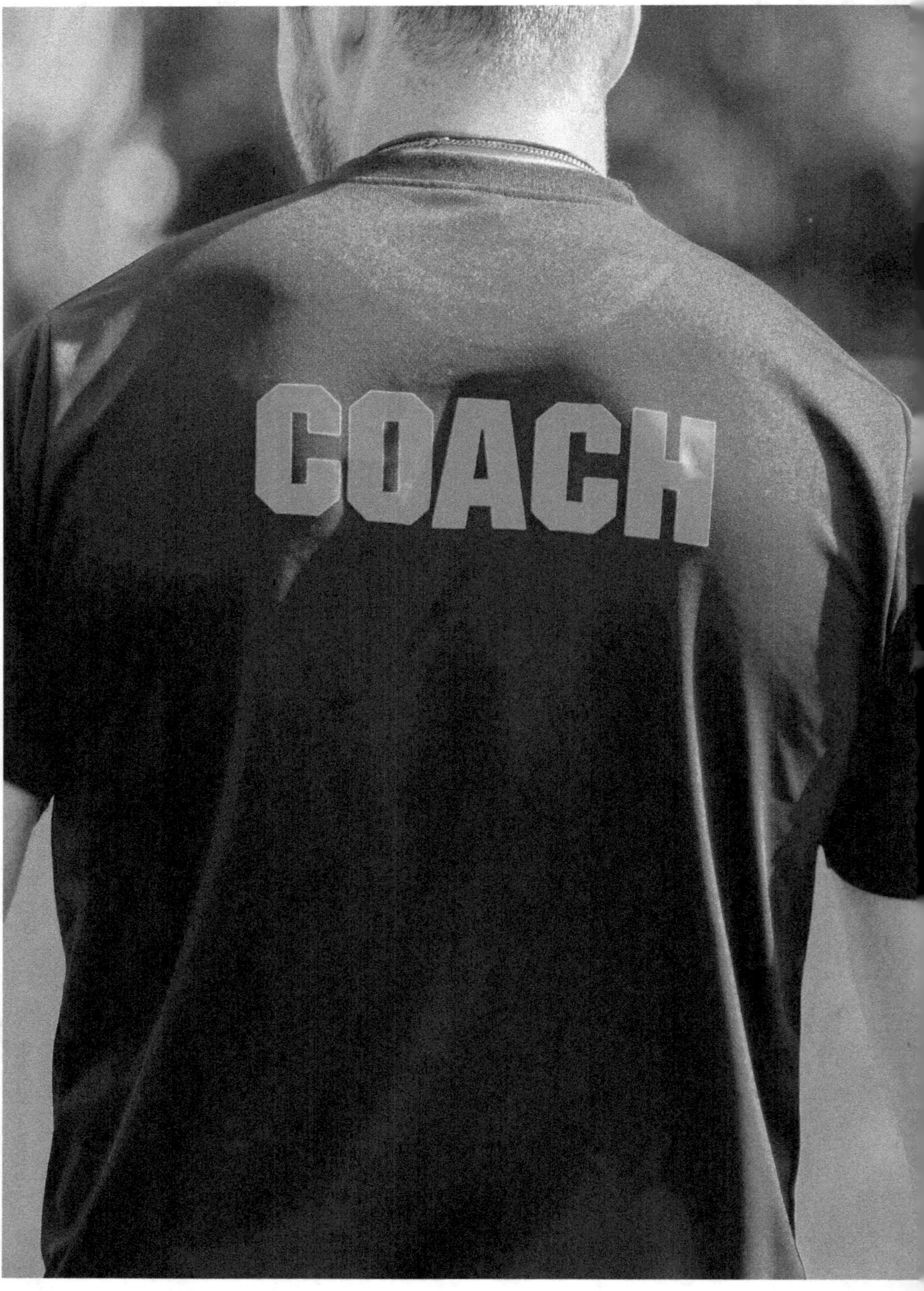
COACH

CH#3
PERSPECTIVE

Do You Believe You Can?

The belief that you can do something is a belief that helps you insanely to perform. In this chapter, I'll show you how important mindset, focus, and ownership are. What's in the heads of your players? And how can you influence that? Show your players that they are moving forward, focus on things that you can influence, and give your players responsibility.

> **You have power over your mind - not outside events. Realize this, and you will find strength.**

Marcus Aurelius

We watch the same game, but still, it sometimes seems like we have seen another game. This has to do with differences in perception. Every individual has their own perspective that sometimes differs from another in a different physical point of view. You sat at the halfway line and saw the play was offside; however, I couldn't tell from behind the goal. Differences in perspective can have another cause.

How your players view, for instance, the usefulness of training, persistence, feedback, challenges, or the feasibility of success, has major consequences for their performance, development, and competition results. Maybe you have players on your team who prefer to avoid a challenge, say they cannot do something, have a lot of trouble with feedback, or continuously ask for your confirmation. Players who are capable of doing much more than what they show but don't show that for some reason. While you probably also have players who are fully involved in the competition, even ask you for specific feedback, and try everything out, even though the chance of failure is high. These are players who get the most out of themselves and every situation. What accounts for these differences between players? You can read about that in this chapter.

The one-mile race has been run since the eighteenth century. Through the years, athletes ran faster and faster, and the record was broken continually. But since 1945, the record has been stuck at four minutes and one second for ten years. For a decade, the improvement stagnated, and not a single athlete ran below that four-minute limit. It was considered impossible that someone could run the mile in under four minutes. The physical ceiling was reached. Until May 6, 1954. After that day, one athlete after the other ran the mile in under four minutes. The record is now at three minutes and forty-three seconds, and it is owned by Hicham El Guerrouj.

What happened on May 6, 1954? That day Roger Bannister ran the mile in three minutes fifty-nine seconds. He proved it was possible to run the mile in under four minutes, and with that, he convinced other athletes. That belief *it is possible to run the mile in under four minutes* changed perspective. Next to a physical point of view, beliefs form perspective. Successful players, especially the best adult football players, generally hold beliefs that help them rather than hinder them. Which beliefs are important in the process of performance and learning?

The most important belief is the belief in one's own ability, also called 'self-efficacy. 'Does the athlete believe he can run the mile in under four minutes? Does the player believe that he is going to perform well in the upcoming training or match? A stronger belief in your own ability nurtures the perspective that something is possible and generally contributes to intrinsic motivation, performance, and development. But, there are more beliefs that play a role.

What other beliefs feed the perspective that something is possible, that a player believes he can? What are the effects of these beliefs on the motivation, performance, and development of young players? And how can you, as a coach, influence the beliefs of your players? For that, I have three keywords: mindset, focus, and ownership.

3.1 Mindset

- Do You Believe In Development?

"The man who says he can and the man who says he cannot are both correct."

- Confucius

During training, the small sided game is due to take place. One player from each team, the captain, moves forward to determine which team will get the kickoff. Fate is settled with a rock, paper, scissors game. One captain sees the downpour again. He is convinced that he is always unlucky in these kinds of games in which luck plays a role. While standing there, thoughts run through his mind like, *this is a game of luck and bad luck, so I will lose again because I am always unlucky.*

Meanwhile, he complains to you and the captain of the opposing team. He thinks it's stupid that they play this game and radiates disinterest. To his surprise, he sees he is showing paper and the other stone in the first round. He leads 1-0. But the game is best of three, and he has to win one more time. Because he's won the first round, our "unlucky person" has become more interested, and his body posture changed slightly. He wonders if he got lucky or if he can really win this time. After a few equal rounds, the other captain wins the second point 1-1. The unlucky person's posture changes immediately, and he radiates disinterest again. His earlier question got answered, he was indeed lucky once and will now lose again. Rather than noticing that his opponent is following the same pattern of shapes, he continues to wallow in helplessness and feel sorry for himself.

The Coach Makes the Difference

'Whatever I do, the other person will win anyway. I always have bad luck. 'That's what happens as the other captain shows paper, and he himself stone: 1-2. As he predicted, he loses the game.

This is an example of how mindset works. A mindset is a set of beliefs that direct the thoughts, behavior, and experiences of a player. Research has shown that beliefs can even influence one's physiology. Beliefs guide your thoughts, and thoughts direct your behavior, and behavior drives your experiences. And in most cases, your experience confirms your belief. It's like a vicious cycle.

The belief 'I'm always unlucky 'steered the player's thought. I'm not going to win this game. His thought then directed his behavior, and he became inattentive, radiated disinterest, and perhaps helplessness. His behavior was not helpful in winning the game. Since he lost the game, his belief got confirmed, Indeed, I have always had bad luck. 'That's how mindset works, that's how beliefs work.

You can break the vicious circle of beliefs by having the player form another point of view or by putting things into perspective. The player expects a bad outcome, so fly in with a good outcome. What if you succeed? In this case, what if you do win the toss? What can you do to help win that coin toss? Another way is to put things into perspective. What's so bad about losing the coin toss? Does losing the coin toss equal losing the game? Because the consequence becomes less heavy, the pressure decreases, and the player is more free and open.

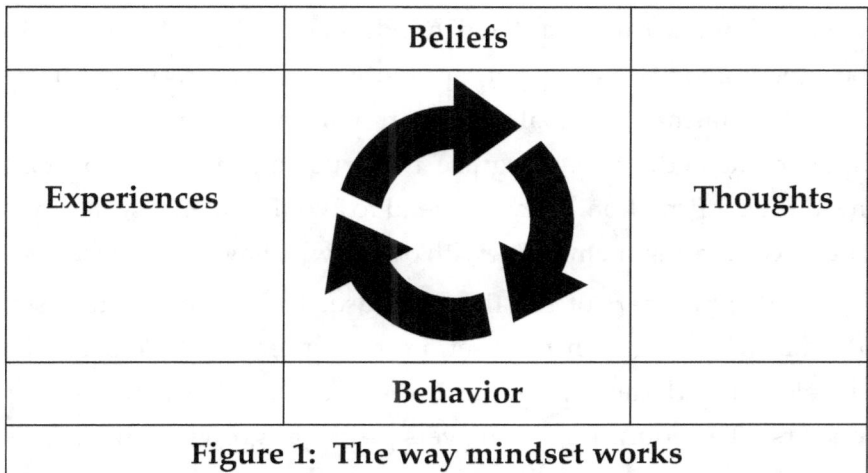

Figure 1: The way mindset works

Beliefs can have far-reaching consequences and be persistent. Even if the experience contradicts the belief, you tend to continue to believe the belief. In line with this lies the self-fulfilling prophecy. That's a prediction that may (unknowingly) lead to that prediction becoming a reality.

In soccer, you, as a coach, are busy developing the soccer talent of your players and improving their performance and team results. Two types of mindset play a role in this, a fixed mindset and a growth mindset. These mindsets were originally coined by Carol Dweck. She discovered a difference in dealing with challenges between ten year olds. For some children, challenges led to tension and were described as 'hell. 'Other kids found challenges great and informative. The children who labeled the challenge as hell, saw the challenge as a moment in which their intelligence was assessed. It contained a risk of failure, *you were smart enough for that challenge, or you were not*.

These children did everything possible to avoid these challenges. The belief that talent is innate and you cannot change it is what Dweck calls the 'fixed mindset'. You have the talent to become a good soccer player, apprentice, or lawyer, or you don't have that talent. The goal of players with a fixed mindset is 'to appear talented.' You recognize these players by their constant need for confirmation. They also tend to avoid challenges, and they prefer comparing themselves with others who have performed less.

The counterpart of the fixed mindset is the growth mindset. Players with a growth mindset are convinced that talent can be developed and can change, and they can become better soccer players. The purpose of players with a growth mindset is developing their talent. You recognize players with the growth mindset for their effort, drive for challenges, and the constant pursuit of development.

The consequences of the two mindsets make the difference in motivation to learn and perform more clearly. The mindsets lead to a different view on challenges, mistakes, and effort, among others.

For players with a fixed mindset, mistakes mean a shortcoming of talent. These players want to appear talented and therefore prefer to not make mistakes. As a consequence, they will take fewer risks generally. Because the less risk, the fewer mistakes. In that way, they may succeed in appearing talented, but they don't develop fully. Also, doing your best is viewed as a lack of talent by people with a fixed mindset. Because if you've got enough talent, you don't have to work hard to be good at what you do. How do you see this in behavior? They don't necessarily give a hundred percent during a workout, don't necessarily want to train extra, or act giggly at other players who behave as training beasts. Perhaps these players come across as talented, but they don't get the most out of themselves.

Players with a growth mindset see effort as a necessity for performance and development. They are passionate about giving a hundred percent during training, want to train extra, and look for opportunities to improve their current soccer performance to improve. They try things and go for a challenge so they develop their talent to the fullest. They view errors as part of that development process and as learning moments. Soccer players with a growth mindset are just as keen to deliver top performances and also regret making mistakes. But they don't dwell on that for long, and they want to find out why things went wrong. This is how they learn more often from their experience.

This difference in responses to an error between people with a fixed and growth mindset is visible in the brain in both children and adults. When being told how well they've performed, the brain is active in both types of perspectives. But when reflecting on the mistakes made, there's a difference in brain activity. People with a fixed mindset have little to no brain activity. They don't pay attention. How different is that with people with a growth mindset? While reflecting, their brains are active, and they pay attention. People with a fixed mindset don't use feedback as a way to learn from it, whereas people with a growth mindset do, in general.

	Beliefs Fixed: 'You either have enough talent for this challenge or you haven't.' Growth: 'Talent can be developed with this challenge.'	
Experience/result Fixed: Easier challenge, well done, learned not so much though. Growth: Difficulty with the harder challenge, but learned a lot.		**Thoughts** Fixed: 'I hope to have enough talent for this one.' Growth: 'Let's see how well I have developed so far.'
	Behavior Fixed: Anxious. Given the choice: rather an easier challenge than a difficult one and might even fake an injury to the challenge.	

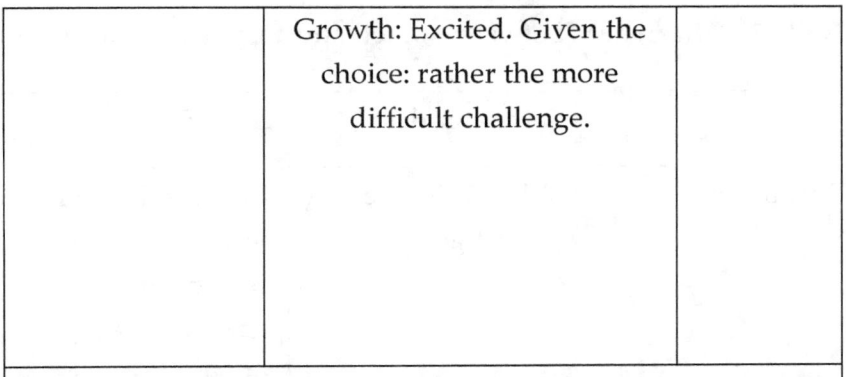

Figure 2: Example of the way a fixed and a growth mindset work, given a challenge

- *Many studies have shown that a growth mindset positively influences intrinsic motivation, development, and performance.*

How is it determined who has a fixed and who has a growth mindset? A mindset is developed through experiences. What example do your parents, friends, teachers, teammates, and coaches set? Since mindset is a belief, it can be changed from fixed to growth and vice versa. How can you, as a coach, stimulate your players to believe they can increase their soccer talent? Make their development visible, share development stories of current top athletes, and give your players specific feedback on their behavior.

Table 3: Differences between a fixed and a growth mindset

	Fixed mindset	**Growth mindset**
Definition	Talent is innate and unchangeable.	Talent is dynamic because it can be developed by learning, practice, and experiences.
Goal	Come across as talented.	Develop talent.
Mistakes	Prevent them! A mistake is a shortcoming of talent.	Mistakes might not be fun, but they're part of the development.
Challenge	Rather not! When there's no other way, rather an easier one.	Challenges show me where I stand and what I can improve.
Effort	Effort is a shortcoming of talent.	Effort is necessary to develop my talent.

Make Development Visible To Your Players

Having your players experience that they increase their soccer talent is an effective way to work on their growth mindset. But how do you do that?

CH#3 - Perspective

It's 3:27 PM. The players still have three minutes to accomplish a keepy-uppy challenge. There are almost thirty players on the pitch as well as six coaches. Two weeks ago, we told the players to keep up the ball fifty times in a row, alternating between left and right foot without the ball hitting the ground. Every player wanted to achieve that goal because the challenge was tough. By now, about eighty percent of the team had completed the challenge. When the challenge deadline passed, six players had not yet succeeded. They were defeated, frustrated, and sad on the field. We again placed the responsibility with the group of players, "Are we keeping these six players on the agreement?"

Within a minute, the decision was made, "A promise is a promise."

That meant that these six players were not allowed to participate in the training session until they completed the challenge. While we started with the training, the six players started working with three coaches. As the training progressed, the players streamed in one by one, which made the team cheer every single time. With thirty minutes of training time left on the clock, the last player completed the challenge. The players left the exercise for what it was because this last player completing the challenge was more important. There was such a party on the pitch that it looked like they had just won the Champions League.

I think a challenge with something at stake is a great method to teach the players what development means and that development is possible. When we explain the rules of the challenge, the players have the opportunity to practice so they understand it. Most players cannot do what we ask of them at that time, not yet. That's where the lesson starts. The player realizes he cannot do something yet. Then he has two weeks to practice for something with high stakes. It is about 'qualifying' for the training session or not. Does the player realize he has to improve himself for the challenge, does he know how to do so, and does he actually practice? Some players get to work and can do it because of practicing at home, at school during breaks, or before training during those two weeks. Some players don't practice enough, if at all, and get the bill presented at the supreme moment. Can you do it or not, on the training pitch, under the watchful eye of fellow players and trainers? That moment is confronting for every player, including the players who have learned to complete the challenge in those two weeks. They all have to prove themselves. When players fail the challenge at that moment, it does not give you a pleasant feeling as a coach, at least not to me. However, the players' sad emotions are no match for the lesson every player learns. Players, namely, learn they can improve their skills if they put in the work needed. They experience that personally and see in others how difficult, not fun, or painful improving sometimes can be. But completing the challenge pays off so much. In addition, every player's victory is celebrated, especially those players who complete the challenge during the training session with teary eyes and a redhead. That gives every player and coach a great feeling. With a sense of 'Yes, we can, 'development is possible.

Another way to visualize development is to repeat exercises periodically. In repeating, you can show your players the difference in performance. They should have gotten better. That is possible with video images, which is objective. But you can also do it during a training session by questioning and telling.

Another way to make development visible costs less time.

We are on the pitch about twenty minutes before the start of a league game, and the players go wild during the warm-up. They are over the moon, coaching each other and cheering. We do an exercise that intrinsically motivates players and also provides them right away with the insight that development is possible. It's a simple pass-and-kick exercise we do in two groups doing the same exercise. The players are positioned in a square with a middleman. In a pattern, they pass the ball to each other. They get to a point when every player in the organization has touched the ball, and the ball has done a lap. During two minutes, they can earn as many points as possible. After a practice round, one yields a number of points in both groups. The goal for the next round is the number of points in the previous round plus one. Players are then coaching each other, "Keep going," "Pass on my farthest leg," and "Play faster," and are motivated to achieve the goal. That succeeds several times, bringing joy and a sense of success seizing the players. Because of the upcoming league match, I do not take time to reflect extensively on the lesson of this exercise. But I have already done that during previous training sessions.

How do you use this exercise to show players that they are making progress through training? After playing a few rounds, you can ask them, "What was your first and last score?"

The last score will almost always be higher.

"It is the same exercise with the same players. How can the score be higher?'

The players will answer that it comes from practice, being focused, or coaching each other. Job done.

What if no progress is made? Then the players need more time to improve. Time is one of the factors involved in development. A seed you plant does not grow into a tree within one day. It needs water, sun, and time. The same is true for your player, and he needs training, focus, and time to grow. For him, the key question is, "Are you willing, time after time, to keep putting energy into your development?" In addition, you may need to refine or change your strategy to achieve the goal.

This is where your role as a coach becomes important. You can provide insight or tips for next time. Tips can be of all kinds, tactical, insightful, technical, physical, motor, or socio-emotional. "What if you hit the ball with the inside of your foot next time? Next time, look around, so you know whether to handle the ball in one or more touches. Next time, coach your fellow player what he can do. Next time, stay calm by looking at the ball instead of thinking about the consequences of the outcome of this match."

What you do is make the cause-and-effect relationship of learning and performance clear to your players. A cause-effect relationship is, for example, 'The more you train, the better you get at it. 'Of course, there are differences between players. One picks it up faster than the other. But in the end, everyone will pick it up, I am convinced. Another cause-effect relationship has to do with winning competitions. If you participate in a competition, you have a chance of winning that competition.

Winning starts with a hundred percent effort in attacking, defending, and transitioning between the two during the match. You train on that during training. An effort is the basis and leads to the improvement of personal performance, such as dribbling past an opponent more often, winning duels, recovering balls, and the number of goals you score. The better the personal performance of each player, the more likely the team will win the match.

- *When you make the development of your players visible, your players will understand the cause-effect relationship. So they can focus on their performance and their own development. It gives your players perspective, nurtures their persistence, and teaches them to think about strategies for achieving their goals.*

Share Development Stories Of Current Top Athletes And Other Role Models With Your Players

Finding out that you are not alone in feeling a certain way gives a lot of people a sense of calm. Even more, if that other person later achieves something that appeals to you. In coaching a high school student, I gave her the assignment to find out how two of her idols have become what they are, "Who do you think is cool, and how did they get so cool?" She discovered her two idols had gone through a lot on their path to success, and they didn't get it for free. One had a few more setbacks professionally, and the other had experienced heavy things in the private sphere. This knowledge led her to realize that she is not the only one experiencing difficulties and setbacks. More people experience them, even the best in their profession. Also, for them, not always everything goes well. They, too, had to overcome obstacles and setbacks. This made the schoolgirl realize that setbacks, mistakes, and difficulties are part of life and it's alright to experience them. Apparently, the world will not end. That gave her peace. She could still be successful, whatever her definition of success was, despite the difficult moments and setbacks of today.

There is a nice analogy called the "Iceberg Illusion." From an iceberg, you only see the top. It may look like a small ice floe, but you don't know what's underwater. That is not visible. That's often the case with the best in their discipline. You can see how good they are when they have reached the highest level. But in general, how they got there is invisible. Some people fill in that invisibility with the idea that the best have always been the best and have never had any difficulties. Otherwise, they wouldn't have made it to the top. If you think like that, you will be amazed when you hear what the path of the best looks like. How did Virgil van Dijk or David Beckham become that good, for example? What is their story? Did they have setbacks? Did they experience difficult moments, and if so, how did they deal with them?

Antoine Griezmann, for example, has been playing soccer since he was five, and he traveled throughout France with his parents to be accepted for professional academies for years. He took part in countless talent days but got rejection upon rejection. Not until he was fourteen was he spotted by Real Sociedad, and he got the chance to develop with them.

Roger Federer, a former tennis star, who won 20 Grand Slams and was the best tennis player for years, underwent quite the transformation in his playing career. Federer was renowned for his calmness on the tennis court, however he wasn't always like that. In an interview he says he went from "A screaming, racket throwing swearing kind of brat on the tennis court to this calm guy you know today." He learned to develop himself in another dimension of playing the game: dealing with his emotions. "I can't stand it watching me throwing rackets and embarrass myself in front of thousands of people in a live stadium, so I tried to change." How did he do that? Partly by changing his perspective on matters, like a loss and making mistakes: "I think losses make you stronger. It's important to learn out of those mistakes. A light goes up in you head, you go like 'You know what, I think I understand now what I need to improve'. And then you become better." Players' development can be multifaceted and sometimes development has to do more with the psychological, emotional or social side of the game. A story like Federer's might align with what your player experiences. And he learns development in those aspects is possible as well.

In addition to sharing stories from top athletes, you can also search closer to home. For many players, the people close to them are an example for them. These examples from *the inner circle* have just a powerful effect as top athletes' stories because your players experience these people from the inner circle up close. They know the ins and outs. They know how hard it was at times.

A single mother who raised four children or a father who grew up in poverty but has built a thriving company through hard work. What lessons and motivation can your players get from that?

> *● When your player realizes that others and many top players have a comparable path like himself, he can learn to cope differently with setbacks. He learns that setbacks are not the end of the world but are part of development and performance. Because of this realization, he can persevere better, becomes less tense about making mistakes, and can play with more freedom and courage.*

Give Your Players Specific Feedback on Their Behavior

The players in your team are unique individuals with various roles in their life. Those roles are separate from each other. Your player can be a very good soccer player but be a lousy student at school or vice versa. He can also be a good person but a bad soccer player and vice versa. Performance on the pitch is independent of the person. Within one role, an action stands in itself. One action on the pitch is separate from the soccer player.

The Coach Makes the Difference

It's Saturday, June 16, 2018, when Twitter explodes. The reason? Lionel Messi. At that time, Messi had already played about seven hundred games for FC Barcelona and the Argentinian national team in which he scored more than six hundred goals. He has won, among other things, nine Championships and four Champions League with FC Barcelona, and he has won five Ballons d'Or for the best soccer player in the world. In 2023 the counter was at seven Golden Balls. According to some, Messi is even the best of all time. He said himself once about his talent, "I started early and stayed late, day after day, year after year. It took me seventeen years and one hundred and four days to become an overnight success." But on Saturday, June 16, 2018, there was no success for Lionel Messi because he missed a penalty for Argentina against Iceland in the World Cup in Germany. The comments on Twitter were not tender."

Messi is overrated!"

"Messi has been lifted over the horse!"

"So Messi is not the best player in the world after all!"

These kinds of messages predominated.

Since when does one action say something about a player? Suppose I would have scored that penalty, would that one successful action instantly turn me into a professional soccer player? Don't think so. Scoring or missing one penalty doesn't tell much about a player. And nothing at all about the person. What does one action say? It says something about that specific moment. The penalty was badly shot because it didn't get in, period. What does a pass that does not reach a teammate and results in a loss of the ball, mean? It was a bad choice because the teammate was not free at all. Or, maybe it was a poor execution of a good choice because the pass was way too far out of direction. But the loss of the ball is about the specific moment in that specific situation.

In the 2019-2020 season, Liverpool loses 3-0 to Watford. Is Watford, therefore, a better team than Liverpool? In that specific match at that specific moment, yes. But, in the same season, Liverpool became champions, and Watford got relegated. So, what does that one match say?

It is not without reason that a team only becomes champion after having played twenty, thirty, or forty matches. And a player is not selected for the team based on one good action but based on multiple actions in multiple matches. Well, that's how it should be.

- *The level of your players is determined by actions and moments over a longer period of time.*

Imagine that during the training, you gave an exercise that didn't go the way you wanted. Normally it does, but not this time. Maybe it was a new exercise, and the distances were not right, there was chaos and little playtime. A waste of those twenty minutes of training, you think to yourself. But what do you think when the head of the youth academy or another coach provides you with the following feedback, "That exercise didn't go well, did it? Is this level not too ambitious for you?"

And what do you think if he said, "That exercise didn't go well, did it? I have that sometimes too. What happened?"

In which of the two comments are you more inclined to defend your qualities as a coach? And which of the two comments invites you out to converse? In other words, with which coaching are chances greatest you learn something from the experience and the conversation, developing you and your players?

Distinguishing between an action in the moment, the player, and the person is important for the mindset of your players. Nobody wants to feel bad about oneself as a person or as a soccer player. If your player believes that one bad action means he is a bad player or bad person, then the stakes are very high, unnecessarily high. You can help him to look at it differently. Your communication is important in this.

Below are a number of coach comments. For each comment, remember, do I coach the person or the behavior with this comment?

"Well done!"

"D'oh, you might not be that good after all."

"Great that you passed the ball with your left foot!"

"Great that you persisted!"

"You are awesome!"

"You weren't fast enough in your dribble; you'd better keep your speed."

"Great that you helped your teammate, man."

Can you see the difference?

With specific feedback aimed at the concrete behavior of your player, you accomplish two things. One, your player learns what behavior you value. This increases the likelihood of him behaving the same way when he finds himself in a similar situation. Two, he learns it's all about behavior for you, and him, as a player or as a person, is not up for discussion. That increases the chance that your player is open to your coaching. He can be a great player or person and yet play a bad pass or game. You want to help him improve his football performance in the next game and don't condemn him based on that one time, but you believe he can do better next time. That is why you give your tips and feedback on the behavior of your player and not on his person.

Defending identity because it was coupled with winning in sports is exactly what former soccer star Craig Bellamy did. Bellamy played at various English Premier League clubs where scoring goals was his trademark. However he was also good at "scoring" yellow and a couple straight red cards. Bellamy thought being angry and aggressive were necessary to perform. He even fought with a team mate during a match when playing for Newcastle United. Why would one do that? His behavior makes more sense when you know his perspective on winning and losing. "Before games I thought 'I can not lose, because then I am a failure." Then the stakes are very high. As he said himself: "How can you play a good match when you put so much pressure on yourself?" This perspective with consequencing thoughts not only put pressure on him and his behavior but on his body as well. Bellamy was injured a lot and his coupling of identity to success on the pitch probably played a role in that as well.

• *Coaching on behavior stimulates the growth mindset, and coaching the person feeds the fixed mindset.*

Table 4: Examples of feedback on the person or the behavior		
Feedback on person	<	**Feedback on behavior**
'You're a natural talent.'		'Great that you passed the ball with your left foot.'
'You are great.'		'Fantastic that you've persevered.'
'You're rubbish.'		'You weren't fast enough dribbling. Make sure to keep your speed.'

Believing talent can be developed, the growth mindset does not equal becoming the very best in soccer or any other discipline. It is not a ticket to the top. It does mean that you believe that you can do something in the future that you can't do yet. You believe you have a chance to achieve something that you have not achieved before. That belief increases your motivation and courage so that you go for that chance. After all, there is no proof that you can't become what you want. No one can predict that, so why wouldn't you explore how far you can get? Maybe going for that opportunity is just as valuable as ultimately achieving your goal. Lots of top players were driven by this, like Ruud van Nistelrooij. He told me he wanted to find out how good he could become and at what level he would be able to perform.

Hard or Soft?

Do you have to be tough on your players? Does that make them resilient? Then Ajax coach Erik ten Hag said about this in the *AD* (19-9-2020), "A lot of research has been done, especially in education, that showed a softer and positive approach has a better learning effect on the current generation. A very critical approach is no longer accepted, really." At the same time, he notes the world around us has become much harder, "Just watch the media and social media and what they can do to athletes. There's so much negative talk. You have to be able to deal with that."

"In the meantime, we have softened in schools and in sports. Do we make the talents resilient enough? I don't judge, but I do ask myself a lot of questions. Being positive has the right effect. This has been proven, but it could also mean that some top talents, as a result, just don't cross the border that top sport requires. Wanting to be the best takes a form of toughness."

Ten Hag advises, "Always look at someone's character." As head of the youth academy of FC Twente, he had the characters of players decompose. "I still do that to this day. Athletes need incentives, and some need a different approach than another. I also find it very important that you coach behavior, never the person. That's the limit for me."

Want to see what effects positivity has? Have a look.

Your brain develops during your whole life

Everyone roughly has the same brain at birth but during life, your brain changes in shape and structure. We call this "neuroplasticity." Every day, brain cells die, and new cells are created. What you do, think, and feel, influences the production of new cells and connections and the functions and structure of your brain. How fast you learn something depends, among other things, on your motivation and learning strategies and the quality of your 'teacher.'

What can you do with that knowledge in soccer? Learning to play football with two feet, for example. Virtually every player is born with one favorite foot but can learn to play football with his non-favorite foot through practice. As he exercises, his brain makes new connections so that he gets better at passing and dribbling with his non-favorite foot. Your players may also start to behave differently because they learn to think differently. You can learn a player who has learned to kick long balls forward, to reach the opponent's goal by dribbling and short to medium passing. This takes time and patience because the old brain connections must be replaced by new ones.

Even past middle age, your brain continues to adapt based on your experiences. The good news is, you can influence that. For example, if you interact with people who see everything negatively, then you become more negative yourself. If you interact with people who speak with an accent, then you will also talk more with that accent. If coach x is an example for you, then you will behave more like coach x. You can teach yourself to behave, think and feel differently. If you have any doubts about this, remember this, do you still think and feel exactly the same way as twenty, ten, five, or one year ago?

> Andrew Huberman, a neuroscientist at Stanford University, researched neuroplasticity, and he presented a two-phase process. The first phase consists of working on the skill with complete focus. The second part is all about sleep. During sleep, the learning experience is being processed in the brain.

In my teams, I have had players with a fixed mindset and players with a growth mindset. And even players with a growth mindset, and myself too, can still be triggered by others or situations that push them towards the fixed mindset. These situations may include doing something for the first time, not solving the challenge quickly enough, making several attempts but still failing, seeing someone else doing better, or receiving feedback focused on your person. Those situations can trigger doubt and the idea that you either "have it or don't have it". These situations are common in a team, every time things are a success or a failure. How do you deal with this in a team? That determines the team culture, which dictates how teammates respond. The culture influences what a player dares, says, and does. That's why culture is so important. You, as ultimately responsible, play a major role in that culture with what you say and do. Do you especially appreciate the result? Or do you particularly appreciate the process? That's a world of difference, which is partly caused by your beliefs. Therefore your beliefs are important. I am convinced that talent is malleable; every player can become a greater talent. But conveying this belief to players and team culture is easier said than done. This requires time and continuous repetition of the message in word and deed. Have a look at how quickly and simply people can influence one another by looking at 'Questioning the herd,' an episode of *Brain Games*.

In my first team at PSV, one of my players showed behavior that matched the fixed mindset. He could get incredibly angry if he lost the ball, and he stopped trying when things didn't go the way he wanted on the pitch. During a game of FIFA, he even walked out of the room when he was three goals down, and he was somewhat reluctant to try new things on the pitch. This player was very good at playing soccer and still is, of course, but at the time, he let his head hang too often so that he did not reach the maximum performance and did not get everything out of himself. I was up for a challenge. In addition to creating the culture, I spent some time on him and his view on mistakes and improving as a soccer player. I told him that if he could do everything during training sessions, he wouldn't become a better player, "Because if everything works out, you will do what you already can, but you don't learn anything new. If you do things that you cannot do yet, you will make mistakes, but you are working to become a better player. I also want you to stop saying to yourself, 'I'm not good enough.' If you make a mistake, you are learning."

In the following training sessions, whenever he made a mistake, I yelled at him, "You are learning!" He gave up many times, said that he was not good enough, and stood on the pitch in tears, but over time it diminished. Until it suddenly changed. He seemed to have found the switch. He had already tried many things that he had not yet done well controlled, but now with more conviction. If it didn't work out on the pitch as he wanted, he no longer gave up, but he made an extra effort. He even encouraged his teammates. He got a lot more out of himself than before and became a better player. He could still be fed up with mistakes, but he was aware mistakes are part of the job and could learn from them.

In addition to my efforts, another change was crucial for the shift in the mindset and behavior of this player. This shift was perhaps even more important because his father's behavior had changed. This father had the best intentions for his son, but he was critical, and he often expressed this in a negative way at first. This father attended every training session and match. With his body language, he left nothing to the imagination, and you could tell if his son played football well or not by just observing his father. After playing soccer, he gave his son his opinion and advice without his son asking for it. That was a burden for this player. This father, however, had a change of mind after a few months into the season. He was still critical of his son but learned to express that in a different way. A way that was more in line with the growth mindset. After playing soccer, he asked his son more questions and only gave his opinion when his son asked for it. He still came to training sessions and matches but stayed more often in the cantine because he wanted his son to play freely and not influence him with his appearance. When he did attend, he was calmer. This father, and other parents of players in that team, told me several times not only his son started to think and act differently, but he himself too.

In that period and in all teams after that, I often used Cristiano Ronaldo as an example in my message that talent can be developed.

The Coach Makes the Difference

It is known how much Ronaldo works and lives for football which brought him to where he is now. He has now played more than a thousand matches for Sporting Lisbon, Manchester United, Real Madrid, Juventus, Al-Nassr and the Portugal national team. He passed the limit of seven hundred goals and became champion in England, Spain, and Italy. He's won the Champions League five times, and he won the Golden Ball for being the best player in the world five times. This quote by Cristiano Ronaldo fits perfectly with the growth mindset, "I feel an endless need to learn, improve, evolve, not just for the coach and the fans, but also to feel satisfied with myself. I am convinced that there are no limits to learning and that it can never stop, regardless of our age."

- *Give specific feedback aimed at the concrete behavior of your player. As a result, your player learns which behavior you value and that he, as a footballer or as a person, is not up for discussion. With patience and tenacity, you can influence a player's mindset and behavior positively.*

Summary

What can you, as a coach, do to stimulate players to develop their talent?

Make development visible for your players.

Share development stories of current top athletes and other role models with your players.

Give your players specific feedback on their behavior.

3.2 Focus

- Complete Or Incomplete Control?

"While you can't control what happens to you, you can control how you react. "

-John Wooden

In line with our need for autonomy, we like to have control. Control over things we do and the things that happen to us. Unfortunately, you are not in control of everything that happens to you. On the other hand, it's not like you have zero control whatsoever over what happens to you. What are matters that you control completely, and what are the ones you don't?

❖ Do you cook kale or order a pizza? Full control.

❖ Does a player follow your tips? Incomplete control.

❖ Do you prepare your training properly? Full control.

❖ The referee's call on the pitch? Incomplete control.

❖ Is your training session going well? Incomplete control.

❖ Are your players developing? Incomplete control.

Table 5: The dichotomy of control	
Incomplete control	**Complete control**
Health	Beliefs
Reputation	Goals
Physical attraction	Preventions

If you let your peace of mind, success, and happiness depend on things you have incomplete control over, then you are dependent on others and external factors. This reduces your chances of achieving success. If what you want to achieve is completely under your control, you will more often have success. You are not dependent on anyone or anything, and you are the only one responsible. Like the Greek philosopher and former slave Epictetus said, "Whoever lets his peace of mind depend on things that are not complete within his power deliberately yields some of his happiness to fate."

The better you and your players understand this dichotomy of control, the better you know what to focus on to achieve the goals. Because paying attention to things you can influence, motivates you and teaches you to use your actions and energy more efficiently.

How do you let your players focus on the things they control completely? Make them aware of their influence, accept what you cannot control, and strive for fully controllable goals.

Make Your Players Aware Of Their Influence

Some time ago, I spoke with a goalkeeper who was sixteen or so at the time. He plays in the higher youth levels of his age group in the Netherlands. He wanted to talk to me because something was not right for him. This keeper blamed himself for every goal the opponent scored. It boiled down to him feeling as if he couldn't have played a good match whenever he didn't keep a clean sheet.

"Your intention is great. There is nothing wrong with that. In fact, I applaud it." I tell him that I think any coach would.

The Coach Makes the Difference

Ultimately it's about maximizing the chances of winning a match. Keeping a clean sheet raises the chances.

Then we started peeling off what contributes to the clean sheet and what makes it difficult. Making saves, positioning, and timing are things that matter. The quality of the opponents, mistakes of team players, referee's decisions, and own mistakes are things that make it more difficult. We list these points. The conversation continued.

"Could it be that you have a good game, but yet your team loses?"

After a moment of thought, his answer was, "Yes."

"Could it also be that you have a bad game, but yet your team wins? Again, he replied affirmatively

"Actually, that's weird," I told him.

He thought so too. While he thought, I took it one step further, "Are you the only one responsible for winning or losing the match?'

After some time thinking, he said he wasn't.

"Are you the only one responsible for keeping a clean sheet?"

Again, after some thought, he indicated that he was not.

"Why not?"

If brains could crack, I would have heard it at the time. The goalkeeper replied, "It is a team sport. You win and lose together."

That was correct, but it was not yet concrete enough for me, "What about the responsibility for keeping a clean sheet? Are you doing that alone?"

Then the penny dropped. He realized he had an influence on some factors and on other less or no influence. We turned to the list once again. By becoming aware of that, the burden on his shoulders was gone.

The great thing is that this keeper, with his fully controllable behavior, can influence certain uncontrollable matters. Think, for example, of his team players' behavior. Does he coach them, or does he not? If he coaches them, he increases the chances of them doing what he thinks is right. Of course, he can also influence his opponent to some extent with his behavior. Is he a goalkeeper with a straight back, chest out, and loudly present, who radiates self-confidence and comes out full on a high ball? If so, the opponents will get a different feeling than when he is a goalkeeper with shrugged shoulders, who is silent and has doubts about going for that cross. That appearance, that behavior, gives the keeper a chance to influence fellow players and opponents.

Table 6: What matters in football can you influence as a player?	
Incomplete control	**Complete control**
Level of opposition	Preparation (rest, nutrition, warming up)
Level of team	Effort during play
Behavior teammates	Coaching teammates
Behavior opponents	Body posture
Referee's choices	Choices during play
Mistakes made	

Table 7: What matters in football can you influence as a coach?	
Incomplete control	**Complete control**
State of the pitch	Training session preparation
Opinions about you as a coach	Training session goals
Your players' development	Coaching during training sessions

- *Give your players insight into their fully controllable and incomplete controllable matters. Let them focus on the issues they can control or influence. That gives them peace of mind and makes them more effective. Moreover, your players, because of this, realize that they bear responsibility but can not be held responsible for everything.*

Accept What You Can't Control

"The opponent is playing mean."

"What a terrible field to play on."

"What a drama queen that player is."

In almost everything you do, you will deal with things that you control incompletely. You can live very healthily, meet the exercise standard, eat healthy, go to work by bike, and still get sick. You can train very good, practice, give a hundred percent, use good strategies, and still lose the match. How do you deal with things that you control incompletely? How do you want to deal with them?

"That referee is really blind, man!"

"He whistles everything for the opponent!"

"What a fool!"

During half time in our dressing room, it is clear who's done it. My players are upset. Despite me understanding them, their behavior frustrates me.

"Guys, the referee did indeed call offside where you can wonder if it was offside. But he does his best, and he listens to the linesman."

"The linesman is not fair at all. He calls with every ball we play deep!" one of the players shouts with frustration.

"That linesman does not always seem to act fair. But," I say, "Do we control what the linesman and referee do?"

The group indicates no.

"So, even though it sucks and you get angry, let it go. That's easier said than done, I know. But think of it as a fact and keep your focus on our game, on your game. Just play the ball a little earlier, for example."

What I tried was to teach my players how to deal with the incomplete controllable matters by accepting them. During the matches, you can do this by showing empathy and reminding your players of the dichotomy. You can train the players on it outside the matches. I have experimented with two training methods to accept incomplete controllable matters.

The first experiment was deliberately bombarding my players with their uncontrollable matters. I had discussed our plan with the staff. We were very curious about how our players would react to it. Prior to the training, I called the group together.

"Guys, next week's training sessions are all about keeping focus. We want you to get better at playing your game, no matter what." In that same week, Ajax lost to Getafe, playing in a very annoying way for Dutch standards. That made a good reference point.

"Do you want to achieve maximum performance, or do you want to let yourself be taken out of your game by matters you can't control?"

Then I told them that we, the coaches, would do all kinds of things to get them out of their game in the coming week. The goal was to train their focus and behavior in learning to deal with matters that cannot be fully controlled. We went all out to frustrate the players. We coached them on every action, cried reproaches, yelled at the players, and talked to them during exercises. In short, we constantly provoked them. Indeed, some players became frustrated and angry. Their teammates then coached them, "Keep calm, keep playing football as you can. They only do this to get you out of your game."

At the end of the week, it was time for a review. In four training sessions, with about twenty players each time, we managed to frustrate a couple of the players. We asked them about their experience and, more specifically on, how they dealt with our behavior. Some indicated they liked it when we were all over them, and others said they kept thinking about the next ball or looked for support from each other.

The second experiment to teach players how to deal with incomplete controllable things was doing breathing exercises. You can call it mindfulness. Several top athletes and coaches practiced and still practice mindfulness. Phil Jackson, who won the NBA eleven times as a coach, is one of the best-known examples. He meditated himself and also taught it to basketball players such as

CH#3 - Perspective

Kobe Bryant, Dennis Rodman, and LeBron James. I also started it, both with myself and with my team.

Rest assured, such a breathing exercise doesn't have to take hours, and you don't need a gong or a carpet. That is all possible, of course, if that is what you like.

What did we do?

Before the training session, I call the group together. Everyone can sit or stand as he likes because we will focus on our breathing for five minutes. I indicate that they can use their breathing as a tool to get calm and remain so. I also state it can be weird to all be silent for five minutes and to hear others breathe. If players have to laugh, I'd understand and don't mind. Next, we count each inhalation and exhalation and do so for five minutes. Do you know what my players told me afterwards? That they felt super relaxed and very focused, and they liked doing it.

That is why I made a video that they can w atch and do at home. You can find the video via the link. 'Chapter 3.2 Breathing Exercise at:

https://www.bauer-vandelooij.nl/bijlage-boek.

During the breathing exercise, thoughts come to mind. You become aware of these thoughts and let them go again by focusing on your breath again. In this way, you learn to accept thoughts that come to you, and you learn to do nothing with them. You learn to disconnect the thought from direct action. Maybe this technique will help you and your players to accept incomplete controllable matters better. If you don't agree with the ref's call, your thoughts and accompanying emotions may become less coercive, so you can regulate them and keep your focus on fully controllable matters,

125

like your behavior. Am I sure to see the effects of this breathing exercise? In any case, it is worth investigating.

> • *If your players learn to accept things that cannot be fully controlled, they are left with more energy for the fully controllable things that matter. They become imperturbable and can perform under various conditions.*

Strive For Fully Controllable Goals

On the pitch, every coach and every player strives to win the match, to be the best, and become a champion. That is not wrong, that's what the game is about, and it motivates us. But those goals are not always helpful. Because you depend on others to achieve those goals, for most people, these goals will therefore remain unfulfilled. The incomplete controllable matters play too big a role. As a result, players feel frustrated or unsuccessful. Or sometimes even worse than that. What they want does not happen. And what they don't want to happen does happen to them. That can be painful. Despite these experiences, they still continue to strive for success. It is, however, possible to leave the pitch without feeling frustrated. Through guidance and practice, your players can learn to strive for success, in which fully controllable matters play a role. Your players will achieve their goals more often, which leads to less frustration and more motivation, as well as a belief in their own capabilities.

We will fill the dichotomy with common goals in soccer. View the goals below and answer the following question, what goal, what aim, fits with the incompletely controllable matters, and which ones with the fully controllable matters?

Table 8: The dichotomy of control. What goals are best to aim at for your players?

Incomplete control	Complete control
Being the best player on the team.	Give your best.
Scoring goals.	Do everything within your power and rules of the game.
Preventing goals scored by the opponent.	Make courageous choices in playing.
Winning the match.	Keep a powerful body posture.
Win 1v1 duels.	Coach team players in a helping way.

How do you set goals which your players have complete control over? An example.

In the preseason, we play a small sided-game in a training session when I walk towards one of the wingers during halftime. He plays at a higher age, U17 at the time.

"I watched you during the game. Are you open to hearing my observations?"

He is.

"In possession, you are almost constantly on the move. You are trying to unmark in order to get the ball, that's great. When we don't have the ball, I saw you defend on two or three occasions."

He nods.

"What makes that difference in the movement for you? Why don't you move if we don't have the ball? "

He doesn't seem to know quite the answer but tells me he wants to save energy for when he has the ball.

The Coach Makes the Difference

"I understand that because you are good at dribbling, making moves, and assisting or scoring goals. You need your energy for that. However, you also need the ball. Without a ball, you cannot show your strength. "

He is thinking.

"So when we don't have the ball, we want it back as soon as possible. So that we can give it to you, for example, and you can do your thing. To get that ball back, it helps if everyone on the team defends. If we play 4v2 and you do nothing as a defender, how big is the chance that you will recover that ball?"

"Not big."

"That's the same with 11v11. If everyone participates, the chances of conquering the ball become bigger. So you participate too. That costs you energy. But if you train yourself in doing so now, during the preseason, you will develop stamina that will pay off during the rest of the season. If you don't do it now, you have to do it during the season, because otherwise, you will not play, then it will be very difficult. So, what counts for you is to keep moving. Both in possession of the ball and when we don't have the ball. Close gaps, put pressure on, and make the playing field small. Keep moving.

How does that sound?"

He nods and thinks it makes sense. Then he asks, "Do you want to observe me again in the next round?"

"I will do that. I will keep track of how often you move in defense. If you find it difficult to do, you can say something to yourself. For example, 'Keep moving. 'That can help you to defend."

In the remaining games, I gave him the percentages of him moving in defense. That percentage increased per game. He defended more and even recovered the ball a few times. This is an example from my time at Willem II, but at DBS, I had an almost identical conversation with a winger from the U19. This is one of the examples that confirms to me that dealing with players of different levels is very alike.

For these wingers, moving in defending is a choice that only they themselves can make. It is a fully controllable goal for them. The more often they defend, and the better he learns to do so, the more likely he is to help the team recover the ball. Wanting to win the game is not a fully controllable goal. The opponents also want to win. It's not to say that winning is a bad or wrong goal to pursue, certainly not. Winning is the ultimate goal of a soccer match. Chances of winning become biggest when your players focus on fully controllable matters, or fully controllable goals, so to speak. In possession, they decide whether to do their best to unmark, whether they are running and whether they are coaching others. In the event of losing the ball, they decide themselves whether to transition immediately, and they are solely responsible for the amount of pressure they put in closing gaps and coaching each other. When everyone does what they can and the chances of winning as a team increase.

To what extent does winning equal success? Because suppose that your players have done everything within their power and the rules of the game, and they end up losing? John Wooden has a great vision on that, saying something like:" Success is a state of satisfaction, because you know you have given everything within your means in becoming the best that you can be."

The Coach Makes the Difference

- *When your players focus on the fully controllable things like their effort, they will be more likely to be successful in achieving their goals. In this way, they learn to act according to their goal. This provides motivation and a stronger belief in one's own ability for future goals.*

CH#3 - Perspective

Summary

What can you as a coach do to have the player focus on completely controllable matters?

Make your players aware of their influence.

Accept what you can't control.

Strive for fully controllable goals.

3.3 Ownership

- How Do You Create Leaders?

"Once people stop making excuses, stop blaming others, and take ownership of everything in their lives, they are compelled to take action to solve their

problems."

-Jocko Willink

The bus was late. The opponents were bigger. He played a bad pass…excuses. Excuses are not untruths, they are often correct, but they are not of much use to you. Even though everyone knows this, including myself, we use them anyway. There is another way of dealing with these truths so that they don't become excuses.

We're having a halftime meeting during a league match. One of my players summarizes the first half as follows, "We play much better, we are much better. But the opponents are bigger than us. In particular, their winger, who is much faster than us. And they score from corners because they are bigger than us!"

After hearing such a summary, things go quickly in my head.

"Good observation! We play well. Your opponents generally are a bit bigger than any of us, that's right. They are dangerous with corners. That winger is indeed very fast. But this is the situation. What can we do about them being bigger or faster than us? What will their coach say when we ask him to substitute their winger, do you think? We can't help it. They will not suddenly become smaller or slower, and we do not suddenly become bigger and faster. What can we do to deal best with this situation?"

The players come up with ideas and strategies for the second half. Not conceiving any more corners is one of them. Only if there's no other option can you defend so the ball crosses our back line, but rather put it over the sideline. The opponent's winger often wins the 1v1 duels with our defender, so we add a defender for extra cover. In addition, the ball pace must be higher so that the opponent will get tired and they will be less fast and strong. Well thought out, here we go.

I try to teach my players to make the best of every situation. That starts with taking control of the situation. That means to take responsibility. Responsibility is not the same as guilt. In guilt, you point to something or someone as the cause of, for example, losing the match, the well-known excuses. Some coaches are good at making excuses. But that is different from taking responsibility for the lost match with your team. In the latter case, you acknowledge your role as a coach in the loss, and you get to work to achieve better results in the upcoming matches. That is taking control of the situation. You can make this visual for your players. They can point to another, the field, the referee or whatever with one finger. But when you point, three fingers always point at yourself. So the situation is like this, but how do you deal with it? What can you do? What kind of plan can you come up with? You could call this 'optimism 'or 'Those who are not strong must be smart.' A while ago, I came across a term that I think is better, ownership. In the book, *Extreme Ownership*, written by former navy seals Jocko Willink & Leif Babin, is explained what ownership is. I have adapted their definition slightly; instead of blaming or whining about challenges or setbacks, you develop strategies and ideas that form the solution to (still) achieve the goal. That is ownership.

What does ownership look like for you as a coach? Instead of blaming your players for not being (soccer) smart, you can perhaps change your coaching. For example, divide what you say into simple and small pieces so that your explanation is better suited to your players. A mistake I often made, and sometimes still do, is that I'm impatient during soccer training. Why don't the players perform the exercise like I want? The solution almost always lies with me. I have the training exercise in my head, but my players haven't. So I have to convey the exercise and the expectations that I have in my head as clearly as possible to my players.

How can you teach your players about ownership on the pitch? You can do this in an accessible way. Prior to a training, you call one, two, or three players to you. You tell them that they are responsible for setting up the goals, the training forms, and training gear in, say, five minutes. They can call their teammates to do this together as one team. Afterwards, you will discuss with the responsible players how they experienced it. How did they go to work? What were the difficulties? It could be their teammates were not very eager to help. What solution did they come up with to incite their teammates? What you do is make players responsible so that they take ownership; otherwise, they don't. In either case, you can discuss what your players have experienced and what they can learn from it for next time.

Ownership on the pitch also means that your players are open to new opportunities. Suppose the team misses its best player. There's nothing else than accepting the lack of that player. But you don't have to accept that you're going to lose because of missing him. What creative plan can you come up with which might have some kinds of pleasant surprises for you?

- *Help your players to develop ownership both in training sessions and in the match. Then they are less likely to become victims of the situation. On the contrary, they become the boss of the situation, and that stimulates them to come up with solutions. This leads to more motivation, belief in own abilities, creativity, and leadership.*

The Coach Makes the Difference

Summary

Ownership on the pitch is important. Encourage that with your team by:

Making your players responsible.

Making your players think about what they can do in the given situation.

Leading by example.

CH#4
Selecting Player

What Are You Looking For?

As a coach, you constantly select for current day's lineup and the team selection of next year. In this chapter, I take you along with research on talent that might shock you.

The best youth players do not reach the top, and the best professional players were not selected in their youth.

Do we actually 'recognize' talent? How do you bring talent to fruition? And what is the role of drinks, drugs, and women.

> Nothing we do is more important than hiring and developing people. At the end of the day, you bet on people, not on strategies.

Lawrence Bossidy

The Coach Makes the Difference

Millions of players play soccer worldwide, and so too in the Netherlands, both adults and children, girls as well as boys. The Dutch FA organizes competitions for young and old. I think this serves two purposes, any player can play soccer at his own level, and every motivated player has the possibility to pursue the highest level. The latter are players who want to reach the first team, possibly on a professional level. That ties in with the goal of every football club, from the fifth division to the premier league. Every club wants to perform as good as possible with their first team.

For this, the clubs needs good players, preferably the best. Bringing in good players from other clubs is a proven method, but not possible for every club. Some clubs lack the resources for that and need to get their first-team players in a different way. In some cases, a club consciously chooses another way. For example, they grow their first-team players themselves. They pay close attention to the development of youthful soccer players and offer promising players a training place in one of their teams to prepare them to perform in the first team. Players are selected for these teams. There are teams like this for different ages and at all levels, from U9 teams and younger from the local grassroots up to the U21 team from a professional soccer club.

Selecting players for a spot in a selection team is extremely complex and not a rewarding task. As it were, you are asked to look into the future. Which player today will be able to make a difference on the pitch in about ten years in an adult league? While weathermen, with all available technologies and data, are having difficulties to predict tomorrow's weather, scouts and coaches are asked to make a prediction about the development and

CH#4 - Selecting Player

performance of a player over a period of years. To what extent is it realistic to ask that of anyone?

Nevertheless, selecting and scouting is an essential part of nurturing players. Hence the presence of scouts at many football clubs. They are the eyes of the club on Saturday along the football pitches. What do scouts look for? Which young players are selected? I will answer those questions first. Then I'll try to find out how well that selection system works.

4.1 SELECTING

What Does Daily Practice Look Like?

"Forecasting is difficult, especially when it comes to the future goes."

-Danish proverb

Most clubs work alike in their selection methods; scouts from the club roam the soccer pitches of their own and other clubs in search of the biggest talent. That's logical if you have to predict which player will make it to the first team later, you'd now expect the biggest talent to have a bigger chance than the worst talent. You want to invest your time, energy, and money as a club in those biggest talents. They are worth the investment.

To find out who the greatest talent is, a scout compares players with each other. Who is most technically skilled? Who shows the most tactical insight? Who has the best motor skills? In short, players who stand out in their achievements are the greatest talents. These are the players who win games for a team and their coach. They make a difference. Many clubs are looking for those players.

What Exactly Is Talent?

There are many definitions and descriptions of talent. If it's about recognizing talent, the following definition fits best.

Definition of recognizing talent, *A talent is the player who is better than other players in the same circumstances.*

'The same circumstances 'are crucial words in this definition. Compare players only with each other if a number of conditions are the same.

Compare a striker with a striker and a full-back with a full-back. Compare players who are not only of the same calendar age but also in terms of physical and mental development. Compare players that have been playing soccer for the same amount of time.

If you want to be able to make the correct comparison, you sometimes need more information. In a friendly match of my team against another professional academy, our striker stood out. He played that game quite nicely, had a share in the match result, and thus aroused the interest of a scout of the other club. After the match, the scout made inquiries with me. Through the information I gave him, our striker was suddenly no longer interesting to him and his club. I had told him that our striker was one year older than most players on the pitch.

He was playing with us in that match because he wasn't very far in his physical development yet, and we found this match a good challenge for him. In our academy, he played in an older age category according to his age. Whether a player is recognized as a talent, depends on the players he is compared to.

Figure: Months of birth of players in Dutch professional training academies.

Q1: 14,909 boys born in January, February or March (40%)
Q2: 10,685 boys born in April, May or June (28%)
Q3: 7,162 boys born in July, August or September (19%)
Q4: 4,891 boys born in October, November or December (12%)

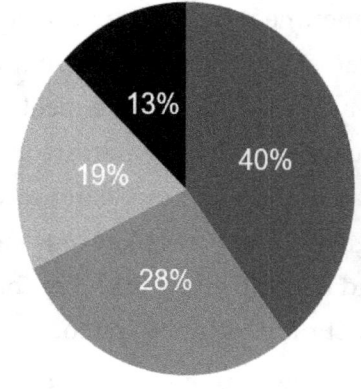

Months of birth from players aged 9 - 19 years old in Dutch professional soccer academies. Data from research done by Dutch FA over a period of 10 years.

Remarkable Effect

The current way of selecting leads to a remarkable effect, the relative age effect. The Dutch FA has researched that effect, see figure. The selection teams of most amateur and professional clubs mainly consist of players born in the months of January through June. Players born between July to December of that same year are underrepresented. You can see this birth month effect to a greater or lesser extent back at each club. The earlier in the year, the player is born, the greater his chance of playing in a selection team.

Does this mean that players born in January are more talented than players born in December? To date, there is no proof of that.

Calvin Stengs (Dec 18), Ryan Babel (Dec 19), Steven Berghuis (December 19), Luuk de Jong (August 27), Davy Pröpper (September 2), and Georginio Wijnaldum (November 11) are some examples of Dutch players born in the later months of the year. With regards to top international players, Kylian Mbappé (Dec 20), Karim Benzema (Dec 19), Raheem Sterling (Dec 8), Gavi (Aug 5), Paulo Dybala (Nov 15), Ilkay Gündogan (Oct 24), and Thomas Müller (Sep 13) are some examples. Diego Maradona, one of the greatest players ever, was born on October 30th. So you don't have to be born in January if you want to be a professional soccer player.

Back to our case in the Netherlands. Could it be more children are born in the first months of the year? It appears not. According to data from StatLine (the public database of Statistics Netherlands), about the same number of children are born each month, between 12,000 and 16,000. Striking detail, in July, August, September, and October, most children are born.

The relative age effect appears to exist in various countries and in various sports. In professional football academies in the UK for example there is an overrepresentation of players born in September, October and November. That's almost opposite to The Netherlands, how is that possible? Because in the UK the cut off date is August 31. So players born in September, October and November are the English equivalents to the Dutch January, February and March born players. In The Netherland the cut off date is January 1st. That tells me the relative age effect encompasses a lot and comparing players with each other based upon a cut off date leads to a skewed representation.

What, then, is an explanation for the relative age effect? The answer turns out to be simple, young people born closer to the cut off date are generally more developed (physically) than their peers born farther away from the cut off date. At a young age, a few months can make a big difference. When they get older, that difference disappears (you will read more about that later).

The Coach Makes the Difference

This brings me to the next crucial question, with the current selection method, are we missing potential top players, and are we giving every player the best chances? Time for further investigation.

- *In the current way of selecting, most clubs opt for the best youth players of today. This leads to almost excluding players at a young age, hence the relative age effect. That way of selecting reinforces the belief that talent can be recognized at an early age. That ensures that players, parents, and coaches believe that a player has an 'innate' talent for football or not, the fixed mindset.*

Summary

From Selection, so far, follow a few points of attention:

Soccer clubs select young talent by comparing players on their age.

Compare players with each other only if conditions are the same.

Be aware of the trap of the relative age effect; then, the talent pond becomes a lot bigger.

4.2 SELECTING

What Does Science Say?

> *"If someone can prove me wrong and show me my mistake in any thought or action, I shall gladly change. I seek the truth, which never harmed anyone: the harm is to persist in one's own self-deception and ignorance."*
>
> -Marcus Aurelius

Players who reach the first team - the highest level - do not always have something in common. Some players are extremely fast, and others are slow. Some players are 2 meters tall, while others just make it to 1.65 meters. Some players are powerhouses, others not so. There are players who like to have all the attention and others who are shy. Some players are very accurate in what they do, and others are sloppy. Some players are super technical, and others run through walls. Some players kick on pressure, and others are bothered by it. Players in the first team come in all shapes and sizes and with various qualities. There is no mold for a first-team player. Everyone and at the same time, no one can reach that level.

Making predictions is difficult. Maybe we'll get a better picture if we do answer the following question, Is talent at a young age an indicator of success later? You will see that from every question, new questions will follow. I will answer them one by one in the light of scientific research.

Is Talent At A Young Age An Indicator Of Success Later On?

Because professional academies start with a U9 or even U8 selection team and they send their scouts to matches of seven- and eight-year-old footballers, it seems there are people who can tell which young player will make it to the first team once they've reached adulthood. A frequently heard statement is that these players have an innate talent. It could be a prerequisite to make it to the first team, and it sets them apart from other players.

If so, you would expect players that enter an academy at the age of eight to play in the academy for years. Maybe one or two players from this talented group gradually disappear because of an injury or something, and a few new players will flow in, but the majority would stay the same. The opposite turns out to be true.

In 2019-2020, Tim Hoppenbrouwer, assistant scouting at Willem II soccer academy, and I did research into the turnover of players within Dutch professional academies over the years. We looked at U19 teams from eight professional soccer academies in the Netherlands and investigated at what age these U19 players had entered the academy. What did we find? Only thirty five percent of the U19 team has been playing in the academy from the ages U9-U12. The vast majority joined later, about sixt five percent. Almost seventy percent of the last group entered U17, U18, or U19 even.

The Coach Makes the Difference

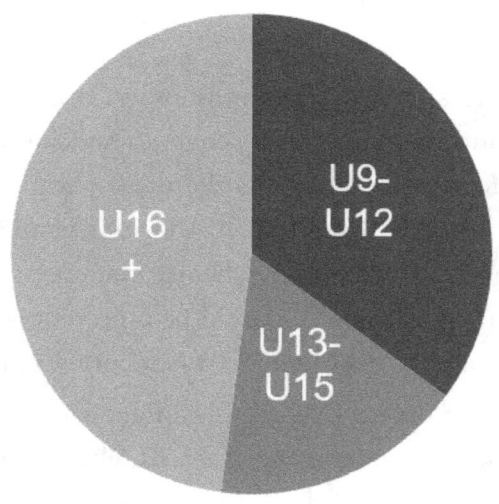

Data from research done as to when U19 players entered professional soccer academies.

These outcomes are consistent with the results of a comparative research done in Germany. Only ten percent of all players who had started in a U11 team from a professional academy were still in the academy at eighteen-year old. Research done by Dutch FA showed that about twenty percent of the existing group of youth players would be replaced, per season.

These are disappointing figures if you believe that soccer talent at a young age is a measure of success later on. This is also evident from various studies. Starting at a young age is not related to success in adulthood. In fact, entering at a younger age appears to be related to early outflow.

Following a large-scale, Australian and Canadian research, the conclusion is clear, being the best youth athlete is not a predictor for reaching the highest level as an adult athlete. About eighty-four percent of top adult athletes were not the best in their youth or did not play at the highest level.

The same is evident from stories in the book *Leerschool Ajax*. Rik Planting followed Ajax's youth academy from years ago. He names three players who, at a young age, were at least as good or even better than Johan Cruijff, but never reached the highest level at a later age. During my visits to the Real Madrid CF and Liverpool FC youth academies, I heard similar stories. When with PSV, stories about youth players who were the very best of their age group also existed, but their names meant nothing to me. These players had not reached the top as an adult.

• *Being the best at a young age can lead to the top, but it is absolutely not guaranteed and certainly not a predictive factor.*

How Is It Possible That The Best Of Today Are Not The Best Later?

The question that arises as a result of the studies above is, why are the best of today not 'often 'the best later?

One explanation is that these players find it difficult to handle once they're no longer the best on the team when they get into a selection team or the first team. Suddenly their fellow players are just as good, if not better. They are criticized by their fellow players and coaches, and they will have to prove themselves. They might have never or sporadically experienced that before, so they have not learned how to deal with them and are at the mercy of their primary reaction, which could be prompted by a fixed mindset. If they respond in the wrong way, they might convey a bad impression. Or they lose faith and motivation to be able to fit in with the top level. In both cases, his chances are all but gone.

Talented players are suddenly no longer special when they are in a selected team, and they are hardly accustomed to criticism. That can be a reason to drop out. Both ex professional football players and research claim: psychological factors such as attitude, work ethic and resilience are very important for (youth) players reaching the first team and top level.

Another explanation for this phenomenon comes from a Croatian research. This research shows that some players mature early. With their physical development, they are ahead of normally mature players (whose biological age is less than half a year different from their calendar age) and have an even greater advantage over late-maturing players, who are physically behind at their age. Within a group of fourteen-year-old players, the 'biological age 'can mark a difference of up to two years.

The early maturers turned out to be over-represented in the selected teams. Not surprisingly, compared to his peers, the early-matured player has the advantage. He is generally more physically and cognitively developed and has, for example, more strength, endurance, and speed. As a result, he often wins more duels, plays longer passes, or has a more powerful shot. Those skills often make him play in crucial positions in the team, and his performance is noticed even more. The early matured player makes a difference for the team and stands out, often also literally, above the other players. That's why the scouts pick him for the team.

The interesting thing about this study is that the fourteen-year-old Croatian players have been followed for years so that it is known at what level they ended up. Only about twelve percent of all early maturers made it to the elite level; they play in the national team and / or in one of the five top leagues (Premier League, Serie a, Bundesliga, Primera División, Ligue 1). About thirty eight percent of the normally mature players reached that level, and as much as sixty percent of late maturers ended up at the elite level. The rest ended up at the sub-elite level, and they play in another (professional) league.

In flow to the highest level, it is precisely the late mature players that are over-represented, that can also be explained. An early maturer can disguise a bad control by winning the duel that follows, for example. However, a late-maturing player must ensure that he learns to play soccer more precisely and faster. His choices, dribbles, and passes. In short, all his actions must be in the right direction at the right time and at the right speed; otherwise, he will lose the ball. Over the years, a late-maturing player learns to play soccer better than an early-maturing player.

The best of today are physically stronger at first. They lose that advantage over the years, while second-best and less good players learn to play soccer better during those years because they cannot compensate for their failures with their physique. Ultimately, the latter group has the advantage.

A head start can also be a disadvantage. A growth spurt nearly killed the dream of a sixteen-year-old Welshman. He played in a professional academy in England, but he had lost his speed. A vote was taken within the academy about the future of this sixteen-year-old. Should they send him away, or should they give him one more year? In the end, there was one vote more to keep him than to send him away. Years later, at the age of twenty-four, Real Madrid bought him for hundred million euros from Tottenham Hotspur.

The Coach Makes the Difference

Had the vote among Southampton's youth coaches at the time been different, we might never have known Gareth Bale as a professional soccer player. Afterwards, it turned out that Bale was growing, and because of that, he lost his speed. By the way, he got it back again around his nineteenth.

• *For how many players did a growth spurt, or a lack thereof, turns out to be fatal? We will never know.*

Can You Become A Top Player When You Haven't Been The Best Player At A Young Age?

There is hope for a player who does not immediately excel. Most top athletes eventually follow a different route to the top. Lots of professional players have been told, as a young boy, that they were not good enough for the highest level. Vincent Janssen, for example, was sent away from Feyenoord U19 because he wasn't good enough. Through Almere City and AZ, he earned a transfer to Tottenham Hotspur, and he wore the shirt of the Dutch national team. Wout Weghorst played in the third amateur level until the age of eighteen. Then he played a year in Willem II's second team, where he did not receive a contract. Later he played in the Bundesliga and the Premier League via FC Emmen, Heracles, and AZ. These stories are comparable to those of, for example, Zlatan Ibrahimoviç, Myron Boadu, Joshua Brenet, Noussair Mazraoui, Jamie Vardy, Dries Saddiki, Antoine Griezmann, and even David Beckham.

• *The eternal substitute in your youth team can, against all odds, later still reach the highest level.*

Does Innate Talent For Soccer Exist?

Although I think genes play a role in development and soccer performance, I don't believe in innate talent. Not in the last place because all the studies I've read about innate talent for soccer conclude the same. There is no innate talent for soccer. Let me put it more nuanced, it has not yet been demonstrated. In addition, genes in and of themselves don't mean anything. Genes need experiences to develop and to show. Robert Sapolsky, a neurobiologist from Stanford, writes that you shouldn't ask what a specific gene does. You should ask what a specific gene in a specific context does. Gene-environment interaction is such a complex process that it is a shame for me as a coach to spend my time and energy on it. At least until someone shows an innate talent for soccer exists. Gianluigi Buffon, a former goalkeeper of Juventus and Italy, allegedly once made a nice statement about this, "You can only measure a player's talent after his career has ended."

- *It hasn't been shown yet that innate talent for soccer exists.*

What Makes It So Difficult To Predict Who Will Reach The Top Eventually?

It turns out that predicting who has the biggest chance to reach the top is quite difficult. Especially because a huge number of factors play a role in the development of a player over a long period of time. It takes years for a talented youth player to get his chances in a first team, and in that time, anything can happen.

- ❖ Will he remain intrinsically motivated to play soccer all these years?

- ❖ Can he deal with setbacks - because he is bound to have them - and does he persist?
- ❖ Can the player and his parents muster to comply with the tough requirements set by some selection teams and academies for years?
- ❖ Can the player resist temptations such as alcohol, drugs, women, or wrong friends?
- ❖ Is the player able to build relationships with others, such as his teammates? He needs them to be able to deliver.
- ❖ Does he fit within the vision of his youth coaches over the years?
- ❖ Will the player stay fit, or will he get injured? Playing soccer for years demands a lot of your body.

These are just a few of the many factors that play a role in the development of a young soccer player. Even if everything seems to be going well, one factor can, and possibly unexpectedly, put an end to the road to the top, as almost befell Bale.

- *Many factors, especially psychological and social, contribute to a young promising player's success at a later age.*

How Good Are We At Recognizing Talent And Selecting Youth Players?

From several large studies follows the same conclusion about talent, which is both realistic and disarming. They conclude that we actually have no idea what to look for and how to unlock talent. In daily practice, there's continuous selection, reselection, and dropouts. In fact, we are not nurturing our talents so much as we seem to be recognizing and selecting talents continuously.

Based on all the studies mentioned, I argue to focus more on training and development of young soccer players and less on talent recognition. In a system where as much as possible young players are offered the best experiences, more players have the chance to develop strength and today's lesser players might surprise us later. Such a system contributes to the belief that talent can be developed, the growth mindset. That ultimately ensures a more optimal development of all soccer talents.

> • *A system with a focus on developing as much children as possible ensures a more optimal development of all soccer talents.*

What Do The Current Competition Formats Enforce?

Better soccer players are distinguished from good soccer players by their brains. Their brains enable them to make the right choice faster and more often while playing. The Dutch FA has investigated the ideal competition format to stimulate those choices in the youngest youth. It showed that a smaller pitch with a smaller number of players leads to more ball contacts and actions. Players have to think, make choices and act more often and faster. The smaller field forces them to find the solution and stimulates, among other things, their insight into the game and their technical skills. That's how they become better soccer players. That is why the competition forms in U9 to U12 have changed to 6v6 and 8v8. From U13, however, matches are played in the same match format as in which the Dutch national team has played the World Cup final three times. Players who just turned twelve play on the same field as adult soccer players. These twelve-year-old players switch to 11v11, from playing soccer on a field of 60x40 meters to 100x60 meters. Take a twelve-year-old goalkeeper with a height of 1.60 meters. That's an above average height for his age. He has to defend a goal of almost 2.5 meters high and more than 7 meters wide. Of course, he wants to avoid goals but has no chance with every shot that comes up to half a meter below the bar. For his fellow players, it is just as difficult. If they want to play on the opponent's half, a distance of about 60 meters awaits them, which they often complete with a sprint. Have them do that a few times, and they are exhausted. To what extent is this competition format suitable for developing technical football players with insight into the game at age twelve? Isn't this match format the same as asking a first grader to do his final internship, do his master's thesis, or solve a business case for a large multinational? In my opinion, it does not quite fit. What does 11v11 as a match form for players of twelve years leads to? Does it lead clubs and coaches to choose the physically more mature players because they are better able to play in such distances? I tend to think so. A team that wants to get to the opponent's goal through passing uses a lot of energy in outplaying the opponents. When they've done so, they are on the center line, and then they have to cross another whole half. The most effective way to get to the goal of the opponent is by kicking the ball into the opponent's half with all the space there and hoping that your attackers are faster than the defenders of the opposing side. This is how most goals are being scored, while this huge space between the goalkeeper and his defenders is rare in adult football. In Raymond Verheijen's view, a good soccer player makes a difference with his head and his insight into the game. The technical, physical, and social-emotional skills are tools. They are in service of the player's game intelligence. That view resonates with me. But what does the 11v11 competition format for twelve-year-old clubs force coaches and players to do? And from what age is 11v11 the most suitable competition format? That seems worth investigating to me. We can turn to England and Spain, where they use different numbers and dimensions.

The Coach Makes the Difference

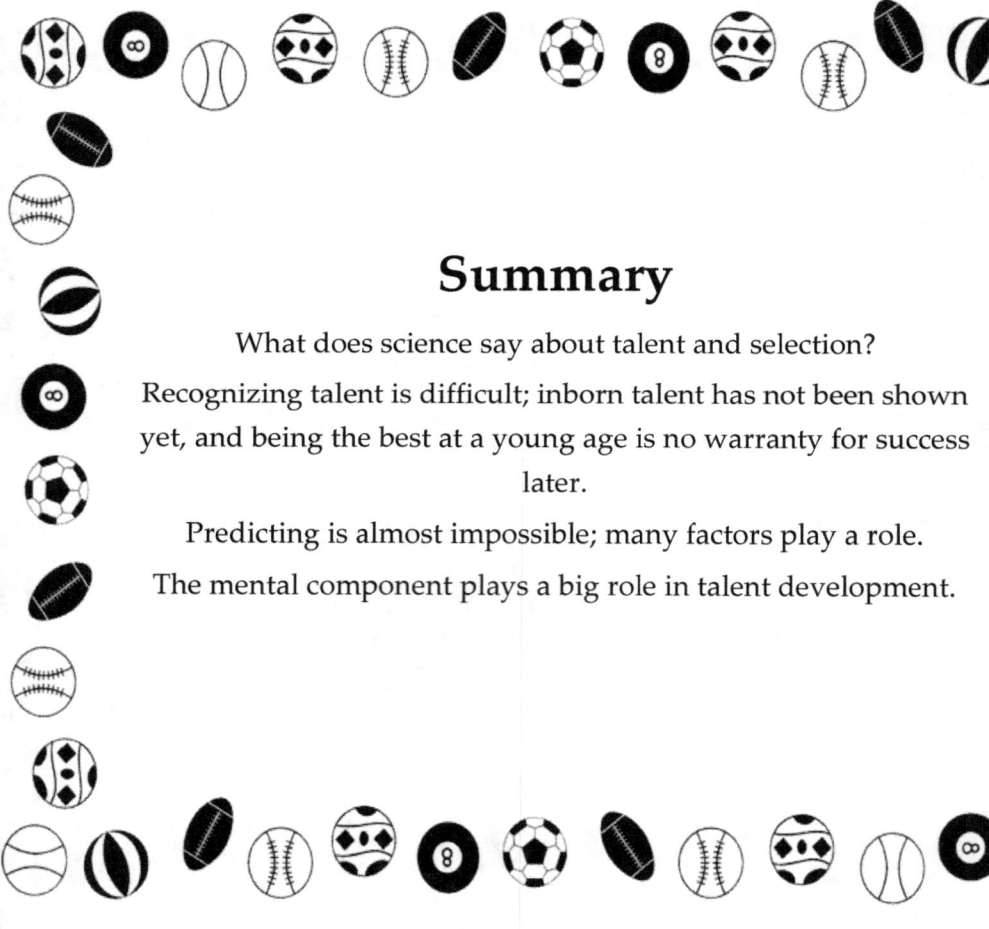

Summary

What does science say about talent and selection?

Recognizing talent is difficult; inborn talent has not been shown yet, and being the best at a young age is no warranty for success later.

Predicting is almost impossible; many factors play a role.

The mental component plays a big role in talent development.

4.3 Practical Tips For Selecting

> *"You will only see it when you get it."*
>
> -Johan Cruyff

You have now read what daily practice is like and what science has to tell us. On the basis of questions that many clubs have, I'll give you concrete advice for shaping your selection policy.

What Can You, As A Coach, Do With This Information In Your Selection Process?

Maybe don't select at all, but give as many young players as possible the best soccer experiences as possible for as long as possible.

Yes, nice, I hear you think, but that's not possible for every club or player. Therefore, in the following paragraphs, I will discuss some dilemmas and questions.

We Only Have One Certified Coach In The U10 Age Group. The Rest Of The Coaches Are Well-Meaning Parents Who Are Unknown With Soccer Training And Everything That Comes With It. Then What?

Maybe the certified coach can lead the training sessions of all U10 players, for example, in a circuit training session. Or, he develops training sessions that the less experienced coaches can execute. An additional benefit is that it takes the less experienced trainers little time to prepare for the training session. Be creative.

The Coach Makes the Difference

Not Every Young Player Is Ambitious. Some Players Occasionally Want To Do A Handstand Or Play Tag. We Bring Those Players No Fun With A Serious Training Session Focused On Performance And Development. Then What?

Differentiate between players based on their intrinsic motivation. This offers advantages for you as a coach. You no longer have a team in which half of the players want to play soccer, and the other half does not or is less eager. With such differences in motivation within your team, it seems impossible to provide a training session that is in line with the intrinsic motivation of each individual player. However, do you have a team in which every player is motivated to play, then you can get started. Of course, there are differences in level between players, but at least they are all willing to give their best. Moreover, in which team do those differences in quality not exist? At Liverpool FC, PSV, or FC Bayern Munich, there are also differences between players in the team. In their teams, a best and a worst player exist too. However, you can achieve goals if you want to go for them together.

At the other end of the spectrum, with players in a team that are less or not motivated to play soccer, you can go for it too. In their training sessions, you often vary between soccer and other games or sports. This gives your players and yourself more fun because the chance is high that your players at least exercise fully. Do share your observations with the parents and the club. Maybe these players would fit better in another sport.

From surveys and conversations with first-team players, experienced coaches, and scientists, intrinsic motivation consistently shows up as an important factor for development and performance at a later age. Having fun playing soccer ensures a

> young player comes to training for years and can lead to him qualifying for the first team. Without intrinsic motivation, he will quit sooner or later.

How Can You Tell Whether A Young Footballer Is Intrinsically Motivated?

Firstly, observe who comes to play soccer. If a player has less or no enjoyment in playing soccer, he will eventually come to play less often, or he might even stop coming. During training, you notice which players radiate fun and who are involved and actively participate. The player who is intrinsically motivated to play soccer, under the conditions that apply to the club concerned, will go the furthest. From research by an Steve Magness, an athletic coach, it was found that athletes who trained most often were the athletes who made the most progress. The more often your players come to train, the better they become.

Is it then possible to predict who will reach the highest level? I do not think so. I believe you can better tell who is not going to make it. These are the players who are no longer intrinsically motivated to play. They eventually opt for something else. As a coach, you can tell whether your approach is successful by looking at how many players keep coming to your training sessions. Therefore, stimulate the intrinsic motivation of your players as much as you can.

What Do You Do If You Have 40 Intrinsically Motivated Players But Only Twenty Spots?

Be creative. Maybe you can rotate players between teams or provide each of those forty players with the same training sessions. Must you select them in permanent teams, then I would first look at their intrinsic motivation and then which of those forty players is most effective in reaching their goals, both on and off the field. Which player creates the conditions to play to his strength? That's the winger who is up against a physically much stronger back but, with various running strategies, gets unmarked. Or he changes position with the other winger so that he is up against a physically more comparable back. And as a consequence, he dribbles more often because he gets the ball more often. Off the pitch, that's the player who lives up to his agreements, who does his best to graduate at school, who has his things in order, and who arrives on time. This player gets things done, even though he may not feel like it, and faces obstacles.

Reaching The Highest Level Is About Playing As Long As Possible In The Best Soccer Academy. Should Professional Academies, Therefore, Include Lots Of Young Players In Their Teams?

Allowing as many players as possible in professional academies would certainly be nice, but in my opinion, it is not wise to do that from a very young age, such as eight, nine, ten, or eleven years. At that age, young players are especially children, who learn through discovery and experience. If children are focusing only on soccer at a young age, I wonder if that isn't too limited for their overall development.

They are soccer players, but they are so much more than that. They are also students, sons, brothers, boyfriends, and the more roles they fulfill, the broader and more profound their development will be. Players who at a young age also gain experience in other sports or activities, for example, in music or arts, develop cognitively, physically, socially, and emotionally more broadly. Moreover, only playing soccer at a young age increases the risk of injury through repetitive and unilateral activation of the body.

CH#4 - Selecting Player

Also, they are more susceptible to lose their intrinsic motivation. That is different if you do various sports. Diverse experiences often lead to more creativity, self-insight, and perhaps even stronger intrinsic motivation for playing soccer. They discover what they really like to do.

What also plays a role in the question of whether it is wise to start at a young age in a professional academy is that it can put pressure on players and their parents. Many young players are not ready for that pressure yet. Most of them are, when they are a bit older and know better what they want to achieve. Moreover, research shows that a lot of top athletes have played various sports or activities up to twelve years of age. From the age of twelve to about sixteen, they focused, on average, on two main sports, and from the age of sixteen, they started to specialize in one sport.

Of course, here, too, several roads lead to Rome. There is no one sacred way to the top. In the short term, players who only play soccer will improve faster than players who also play other sports or do other activities. Nevertheless, in my view, that choice is up to the player and his parents. They choose together what they feel most comfortable with in the upbringing of their child. A professional academy from U13 or maybe U12 seems most ideal to me, from a scientific perspective.

What If You Must Select Players At Your Club? Then What Are You Looking For?

Look in particular for things that tell you something about the growth opportunities of a player. These could be things that help to improve his soccer performance, and that stimulate his development as a player and as a person. On this level, I have been inspired by the Navy Seals and their selection methods.

165

The Coach Makes the Difference

In the army, navy, and special forces, stakes are highest. It is a matter of life and death. One lesser performance, and it's possible that it's over. In soccer, losing the game is the worst thing that can happen. Another chance next week. The fascinating thing is that in defense, they don't so much look at who is the best soldier now. They especially look for those who are 'mentally 'so strong – or can become so – that he learns to complete any mission, whatever the circumstances. They look for people that can act according to their goal that provides reliability.

Therefore, look for more than just the best player of the moment. Look especially at his intrinsic motivation and whether he acts according to his goal; those factors give you an insight into how strong the player can develop. Can the player, given the circumstances, adapt in such a way that he performs and develops optimally? This is hard to see during a match where his coach may have given him instructions.

My advice to scouts and coaches consequently is to visit the training and have a chat with the coach, with the parents, or even with the teacher at school of the player you have in mind. John Wooden did so in recruiting basketball players for his UCLA basketball team. Should selection training sessions be within your possibilities, then make it difficult for the players, and give them a big challenge. How does each player react? Who blames others, gives up, or is suddenly injured? Who takes the lead, sets an example, and acts according to his goal?

The following questions form a kind of checklist for myself in judging young players:

- How often does the player come to play soccer?
- Does the player give me the impression that he is intrinsically motivated to play soccer? Does he actively participate in playing, is he focused and engaged?
- How often does the player act towards his goal, both on and off the pitch?
- To what extent is the player curious? Does he dare to try new things?
- To what extent is the player eager to learn? Does he practice for himself, does he react proactively to feedback, or does he come up with questions himself?
- Does the player believe in development?
- What is the core quality of this player? What makes him a good soccer player?
- Is the player aware of his core quality?
- To what extent can the player reflect?
- Do other players play the ball to this player?

How to Develop Talent?

At the beginning of this chapter, I gave the definition of recognizing talent. In my view, it is more interesting to discover how each of your players learns, how to strike a chord within him, what good teaching methods are, and how you can reconcile those things. That is why I now give you the definition of talent development, which in my view, is much more relevant to youth education.

Talent Development Definition:

Aptitude x experience x ambition x discipline x willpower In terms of development, you mainly look at the player who is intrinsically motivated to develop themselves to the fullest. The following five factors influence that: aptitude, experience, ambition, discipline, and willpower.

- Aptitude is the genetic profile a player has received from his parents. Aptitude comes to fruition (or not) from all experiences he has gained up to the moment you start working with him.
- Experiences are things the player has learned from previous coaches but also things he has experienced on the pitch. That's why he's learned to play in a certain way.
- Ambition is what the player wants to achieve.
- Discipline is to what extent the player works towards his ambition, to which extent he acts on his purpose.
- Willpower is about the player's behavior when the going gets tough. Will he then continue to act on his purpose? The question, 'How badly do you want to achieve your goal?' leads to self-insight within the player.

In talent development's formula, aptitude and previous experiences are a given that you can no longer change what has been but you can offer your player new experiences. In addition, his ambition, discipline, and willpower are changeable. You can make your players aware. For example, mirror your player's behavior to his ambition. Are they in line with each other? Reflect on situations and think of strategies together for future situations so that you help your player to increase his willpower. The stronger the ambition, discipline, and willpower of your player, the more likely he is to improve his football performance and becomes a bigger talent. As far as I'm concerned, anyone who is intrinsically motivated can become a talent, and time will tell which players are the biggest talents. Your role is to get the most out of your players to fit with their ambition. You can influence them both negatively and positively, but in the end, it is up to the player what he does with it.

- *In summary, you can say that selecting and training good players resembles a self-fulfilling prophecy. The best training leads to the best players. The more young football players selected for the best football training, the bigger the number of good soccer players becomes and the better the best soccer players are when they've reached adulthood. More or better talents are not suddenly born. It is not a matter of drafts. We have the key in our own hands, and we determine how many and which players we select for better training spots.*

Summary

What's important when selecting players?

Do not select. Give as many players as possible the best possible training programs for as long as possible.

Base your choice on the growth opportunities of the player. Intrinsic motivation is essential for performance and development.

The best soccer education leads to the best players. That's why talent development is more important than recognizing talent.

CH#5
SHARE YOUR VISION

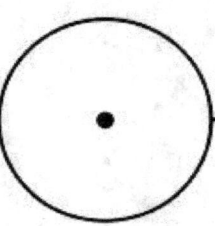

How to Create Clear Expectations?

The Netherlands has seventeen million national coaches, and you might know this expression. However, most coaches are not so much bothered by the media and the public. But you, too, have to deal with expectations and opinions from others. From your players, your club, and your players' parents. Let me show you in this chapter how to stay upright and how to involve everyone in a constructive manner.

Just like your players can't do it alone and they need each other to perform, so do you as a coach need others to perform at your best. Sometimes you lead, and sometimes you need guidance. Therefore, make good agreements that are in line with the club and your team and ensure the right expectations between the parents of your players and yourself.

> **Action without vision is a nightmare. Vision without action is a dream.**

Japanese saying

5.1 What Club Appointments Do You Make?

"Real gold is not afraid of the furnace."

-Chinese Proverb

First of all, you align your ambition and vision with the club you work for. What course is the club heading? What do they expect from you, and what are you allowed to expect from the club? The more clearly you know for yourself what you want, the easier it becomes to find alignment with the club or to find out it's not there.

Topics you can talk about are:

- What makes a good youth coach?
- Is winning or developing the starting point?
- What is the way of playing soccer, the way of playing?
- What requirements should a training meet?
- To what extent does the club support you?
- What does the club offer if you have little experience and you need guidance? Is there an internal or external coaching course in which you can participate?
- Does the club periodically organize a meeting between the technical committee and its coaches?

If those folds have been ironed out to mutual satisfaction, it helps to schedule a meeting with your staff (if you have one) at the beginning of the season. With them, you can share your ambition and vision and discuss the cooperation. What do you like about the collaboration, and what are your staff members' wishes? What do you expect from your staff and what can they expect from you? The agreements you make will help you lead your team.

- *Making agreements with the club ensures a clear club culture in which you will work together. The vision, norms and values, and playing style are clear. This gives direction for both your behavior as well as from the club.*

5.2 What Team Agreements Do You Make?

"Where there is unity, there is always victory."

-Publius Syrus

Norms and values prevail in teams and organizations. There's a certain culture. Before you go to the drawing board for training sessions, it is good to first determine the norms, values, agreements, and culture with your players as a team. What does every player want? What does the team want? Is there a goal for the season? How do you want players to interact with each other? How do the players interact? What is the procedure if someone is late? What happens if a player doesn't have all of his stuff with him? How do we react when someone makes a mistake? Discuss these kinds of things with your players at the start of the season. Schedule a team meeting before or after a training session instead of one, create clarity for everyone, and take the first step towards becoming a team.

Questions you can discuss with each other are:
- What characterizes a team?
- Who is responsible for the materials? Are the coaches or the players responsible for them?
- Will the best eleven play, or will everyone get playing time?
- How do we want to deal with each other when things go wrong?
- How do we want to interact with each other when things go well?

- What do we do when we are in top form?
- Suppose your teacher at school asks about our team. He sees you're proud because you are part of our team. What things do we do that makes you proud?
- What has to happen in the team that makes you no longer want to be part of this team?
- What should we always be able to hold each other accountable for?
- What do we do so that you know we can trust each other blindly?

"The relationship between hard work and achievement is important to him. Making mistakes, playing badly, that's possible. That's fine as long as you give it your all you have in you," says footballer Adam Lallana about his former coach Jurgen Klopp. That is also what I stand for as a coach and what I strive for with my players. I share with them how important I think hard work, just you doing your best, is, and I put that into practice with, for example, playtime and captaincy.

In terms of playing time, I tell my players that each player will have more or less the same playing time. They have to earn that, though, by giving 100% of what they've got almost always. If I was under the impression a player did just that, which is subjective, then the player got his playing time. But sometimes, I did something where my subjectivity played no role so that my players were less dependent on me and more on themselves. Players could prove themselves through a challenge. In that challenge, on the last training session or prior to the warm-up, each player was given the opportunity to fight for a spot in the line-up or play the entire match.

An example.

With a league game 8v8 coming up, I have ten players. We play four parts, meaning that during each part, two players are on the bench. That also means that two players can play the entire game. To determine who will play the entire game, we do a push-up challenge. Which two players do the most push-ups? Those two play the whole game. I varied with the challenges on a technical, physical, cognitive, and social level so that it was as fair as possible. Some players have qualities more on the physical side, and others more on the cognitive side. At least that's what you'd expect

But what I noticed is that it doesn't matter that much. There was, of course, some variation in the winners, but generally, the same players rose to the top. It says more about the will of a player.

Examples of other challenges: Who can keep the ball up most often, who solves a sudoku the fastest, and which pair works best together in making the most passes?

In terms of captaincy, I wanted to strengthen the relationship between hard work and making success tangible. Together with players and staff, we determined which skills a captain should possess. We agreed on: leading by example, helping teammates, and taking the initiative. Before a league game, I asked my players, which player, based on his behavior during last week's training sessions, had deserved to wear the captain's armband in the first half. The chosen captain was then allowed to choose an assistant captain who would support him on the pitch. Then we agreed we would decide during half-time who would become captain in the second half. Of course, this is more subjective, but that's what I find fantastic in this case. Players are free to choose who they wish their captain and their leader to be because they have to listen to him.

CH#5 - Share Your Vision

- *Making agreements with the team ensures a clear culture where you will work together. The vision, norms and values, and playing style are clear. This gives direction for both your actions and those of your players.*

5.3 WHAT AGREEMENTS WITH PARENTS DO YOU MAKE?

"The person who tries to travel on two roads at once gets nowhere."

-Xun Kuang

Finally, there are your players' parents. They are very important because they raise the kids who play on your team. I am aware that parents can be a pain in the ass, like those parents who want to have their say in anything. Luckily in my experience, the parents of my players weren't like that. On the other hand, do you realize that as a coach, you can also be a pain in the ass for parents? That happens, among other things, when you promise things but don't live up to them. I experienced that in my second year at PSV. I had told the players and parents in meetings about the norms and values that I wanted to use in the team. Then staff members were late for the next game. Because my parents saw me as ultimately responsible, they spoke to me about it. 'If you want our son and us to stick to the standards and values, you have to lead by example,' was the purport of their feedback. They were right. As a staff, we discussed the norms and values and how we were an example for our players and their parents. Luckily, this one time turned out to be an exception, and afterwards, we set a good example.

You have a major influence on the cooperation with your players' parents. Just like with the club, your staff, and your players, you can involve the parents in your ambition and vision. Share them with them so you get clear mutual expectations. Organize a parent meeting at the beginning of the season. After this meeting, parents know how you want to work, what you expect from them, what you expect from the players, and what they can expect from you. Also, in this case, the agreements you make, offer peace and clarity to everybody. In addition, you can address each other on behavior based on the agreements. That's easier than addressing someone for behavior without prior arrangements.

Topics to discuss with parents include:

• What is my vision on soccer? Are we going to learn to play soccer, or does the way we play doesn't matter as long as we win?

• How do I deal with the players / your child?

• On what basis do I divide the playing time between players during matches? Do the best play the best, or does everyone have playing time?

• What are the standards and values around training sessions? Do I want parents on the sideline, or are they allowed to come onto the pitch?

• What happens if a player is not fit?

• What if a player is late?

• What do I expect from parents? For example, is it practical to draw up a transport plan?

• What do I expect from the players?

• What can players and parents expect from me? At what times can they reach me for questions or comments?

• Do we want to participate in tournaments?

In my experience, these practicalities may not be the most fun in your work as a coach, but if you do them right, you will hardly have to spend time and energy on them. The agreements are in place.

An agreement I made with parents was that players themselves signed off for training or a match with me. Parents were allowed to check whether their son signed off, but I heard from the player when he didn't come to play. The explanation here is that your son will become self-reliant in this way.

Another agreement was, 'let me explain'. Do you have any questions or any ambiguities, come to me and let me explain. Why would you explain to parents why you do the things you do? There's two reasons for me. On the one hand, it provides peace of mind. If there is ambiguity, sooner or later, parents will start looking for an answer themselves, and chances are their answers will not be positive. Before you know it, they're dragging their child or other parents with their negativity. You don't want that. By listening to parents and removing their doubts, clarity is created. They can give the same message to their son as you. That doesn't mean they will always agree with you, that's fine too, but at least it's clear. On the other hand, it is a control for myself. If I can explain it to the parents, then what I do fits with what I stand for. When I couldn't explain, I knew I had to think more about it. That keeps me sharp. This appointment also contributed to my connection with the parents of my players. Do you want to change parental behavior?

Then there are at least two ways that are effective. The most powerful way is to pass your players' opinions on to their parents. For example, have your players write down, anonymously, what behavior of their parents they dislike or wouldn't like. On another piece of paper, you have them write down which behavior of their parents they like or would like. You share this information with the parents. That's a true reality check.

CH#5 - Share Your Vision

Another way is by setting an example yourself every time, both on and off the pitch. In support of this, you can send inspiring articles or videos. In the beginning, I made the mistake of wanting to convince my parents, which was less effective. What works better is sharing knowledge and giving them the space to form their own opinion. For example, on various occasions during the season, I sent them an article or documentary with the message, 'If you find talent development interesting and you have half an hour, you will find this worth a watch.' When you do this, a number of parents still won't be interested, but what several parents told me was that they found it interesting. They thought about it, and some even changed their perspective and behavior because of it. Maybe for the parents of your players too.

- *By making agreements with the club, players, and their parents, you create a culture of interacting with each other. This gives peace of mind for your players and yourself to perform optimally, develop, and win competitions. In addition, it keeps you sharp and contributes to your connection with the club, your players, and their parents.*

Summary

How do you create the right expectations?
Make agreements and set goals with the club.
Make agreements and set goals with your players.
Make agreements with your players' parents.

CH#6
TRAINING

How Do You Improve Performance?

Making many hours on the pitch contributes to better performance, but it is mainly the quality of those hours that counts. In this chapter, I help you form a practical vision for training. How do you set effective goals? How to fit in with what players can already do? How do you challenge them? I give you three didactic principles for a successful training session, and we'll have a look into a couple of good exercises.

> **Amateurs call it genius, masters call it practice.**

Thierry Henry

According to the dictionary, training means 'practicing systematically in a branch of sport, especially before a competition' but also, 'practice in a certain skill.' In my view, the purpose of training is twofold; on the one hand, you want to prepare players for the match so that they can perform optimally during the competition. This goal is short-term. On the other hand, you also have a long-term goal because you want to raise the performance level of players so that they become better players in the long-run. You can fulfill these goals in many ways because, in soccer, you can train so many things. But, what is training? And how do intrinsic motivation, belief in one's own abilities, and culture go along with training?

As far as I'm concerned, training is acting towards a goal and getting better at it. It is obtaining a firm cross pass, better unmarking, and getting more often in the opponent's box, you name it. It takes time to perform better; every top soccer player and each team trained for many hours to become as good as they are now. The number of hours of training contributes to improving performance. However, the quality of those hours is even more important. In there, intrinsic motivation plays an important role.

A player who is intrinsically motivated is eager to learn and is open to it. How different is it with a player who is not motivated? Yet intrinsic motivation does not equate to learning. Because a player can really want to train, but if he doesn't have the right strategy, for example, to be better at passing, he will not improve his performance, and he won't learn. So why does intrinsic motivation make learning more effective? Because learning takes effort. It is often impossible to learn something in one go. It takes time, multiple attempts, patience, focus, perseverance, and sometimes, literally blood, sweat, and tears. A player who is not intrinsically motivated will eventually refrain from doing so. He stops his efforts earlier, does not want feedback, or does not seek the right strategy to learn something compared to the player that is intrinsically motivated.

What also plays a role in this is the belief in one's own ability. A player who believes he can or can learn something continues if the first times were unsuccessful. That player believes he can develop despite the setbacks and keeps looking for strategies that do work. How different that is for a player who thinks in black and white; you have it, or you don't. If you believe you don't have it because it failed a few times, why would you continue? Therefore, beliefs and, in particular, the belief in one's own abilities are so important.

In addition, it is important for a player not to feel too stressed. Too much tension paralyzes the brain causing the player to be unable to store new information. This lowers the learning effectiveness. The culture within the team has an influence on that stress and that tension. How do teammates and the coach respond during a training and learning process? A culture in which a player is laughed at, blamed for having too little talent, or requested to stop trying if his attempts fail has a different impact on that player than a culture in which a player is encouraged, challenged, and helped when his attempts fail. That's why culture is so important. A culture with high expectations is good for learning and improving performance as long as you properly support and guide the player.

In a good training session, intrinsic motivation, belief in one's own abilities, culture, and training content come together. How do you determine that content? How do you provide training? Of course, every player learns in his own way, but there are some universal guidelines. I will spotlight them one by one. Think from big to small in your training goals, align with what your players already can focus on the right strategies, and use didactic principles.

In a type of training where intrinsic motivation, belief in one's own abilities, culture, and training content coincide, players, learn more effectively.

Training

Think from big to small

6.1 How Do You Set Effective Training Goals

"Start with the end in mind."

-Stephen Covey

In soccer, a distinction is made between four main moments, attack, and transition from attack to defend, defend and transition from defend to attack. Soccer skills are often also distinguished on a tactical, technical, physical, and social-emotional level. You are spoiled for choice in what you want to train.

How do you decide what to train? Think from big to small. What is the vision of the club, and what are the standards and values? How do they translate to your team? Take this with you and first determine what you are about, for example, where you want to be within a year. Start with your playing style. What kind of soccer do you want your team to play? For example, do you want to play attacking soccer à la Guardiola, more on the counter like Mourinho, or do you want to play like the old-fashioned English kick and rush? Do you want to build up and play with passing towards the opponent's goal, or do you want to kick the ball long and see what'll happen? Do you want to put pressure on the opponent when they have possession of the ball, or would you rather have them come?

Then you determine where your players are now and what the gap is between where you want to go and where you are now. What can your players already do? What can't they do yet? Once that is clear, the key question follows, 'How do you achieve the goal?'

CH#6 - Training

There are coaches who have a training schedule for the complete season, and there are coaches who think about what to train fifteen minutes before the training session starts. Depending on what suits you and the time you have, you can decide how to prepare your training sessions. I do always advise you to keep in mind your way of play and to think from big to small in your training sessions.

That's why I often have one to three training goals on which we train for one or two weeks. This method is comparable to what they would call a 'sprint' when working agile. Why would you want to do it this way? Because it directs your training sessions and coaching. In addition, your players know what they will be training in the coming week or two weeks.

A lot happens in playing soccer, and at no level do players exist that play perfectly, so you can observe and coach on everything. In my experience, that is less effective. Working with a focus on goals and skills ensures that I have a clear focus, and so do my players.

That is why it is often more effective to do a limited number of exercises in a training session. If I train for one hour, I do a maximum of two exercises and a final game, small-sided or match. If I train for an hour and a half, then I do a maximum of three exercises plus a final game. I'd rather have fewer exercises in my training sessions so that I have time to work specifically on the training goals and build intensity in the exercise. Personally, I feel more exercises tend to lead to less focused work on the training goals. And this often leads to lesser intensity of the training session. Cruyff trained for a maximum of one and a half hours and said, " I like to train short but intense. The longer you train, the more likely you are to slack."

Also, in designing tonight's training, you work from big to small. What do you want your players to do better after training? How do you design your exercises? Consider, for example, the number of players during the match, like 11v11, and decrease the numbers in the exercises so that more repetitions will take place. Partly for this reason, the coherence between your exercises is important because the better the cohesion, the stronger the learning transfer between exercises and from training to the match.

You trained on one goal for a week, and then what? You can repeat this goal in, for example, three weeks. There's a good reason for repeating. Studies in schools have shown that students learn more effectively in the long term when learning experiences are disseminated instead of going through one skill once and never coming back to it. This is the so-called 'spacing effect'. This also applies to sports. It has to do with how our brains work. If your player is training, his working memory is busy with the skill or the tactical idea. At that point, he may be able to do what he trains, but has he learned it? In order to learn, it is important for the skill to be stored in long-term memory. To make that happen, doing something once is less effective than spacing the learning experiences. Offer a skill or tactical idea therefore periodically. Repeat every few weeks, and raise the bar per every repetition so your players are improving their performances in a sustainable way. Remember what Huberman said about learning, it's a two step process, tell your players to sleep well so that your players' learning process is as effective as possible.

This also means that after a short period of time, you will not be able to judge your players' development. Development after a few weeks seems beautiful but is often short-lived. To see sustainable development, give a player more time, maybe half a year to a year.

In addition, it works great to vary the way you train the skill or tactical idea. For example, train the technique on different surfaces such as grass, artificial grass, stone, sand, you name it. You can train the same tactical idea in varying contexts, such as in number of players underload or overload, with ten or eighteen players, with one goal or more goals on the pitch, and so on. Variation leads, according to professor of neuropsychology Erik Scherder, to better connections in the brain, making players learn and perform better.

- *Training sessions with a clear focus, high intensity, variation, learning transfer, and periodic repetition demand the maximum from your players. This provides intrinsic motivation, a stronger belief in own abilities, more effective learning, and better performance.*

Summary

How do you set effective training goals?

Think big to small when setting your training goals.

Club vision -> way of play -> training -> exercise.

Choose up to a few skills or tactical ideas within one training session you Coach and repeat this periodically, this lasts better in the brain.

Add variation in your way of training. This makes stronger connections in the brains of your players.

6.2 How Do You Align With What Your Players Can Already Do?

"I listen, and I forget. I see, and I remember. I do, and I understand."

- Confucius

To achieve your training goals and develop your players, it is important that you align with what your players already know and can do, because we learn based upon what we already know and can. How do you do align with what your players already know and can? For example, make sure your players understand the connection between the exercises and the way of play. That coherence can be made clear in several ways.

Connect With What the Player Can Already Do and Know

With a player who has trouble passing the ball over 10 meters, you can not train on a 40-meter pass. You can't train with a player who is not completely fit the way you can with ones who are. Training under the highest pressure with a player who has never felt pressure before training is not smart to do. Or at least, it is all possible, but to what extent would it be effective? Estimate what your players can do and adapt accordingly.

Especially on the tactical level, your players learn more effectively when you align with what they already know and can do. Activate their foreknowledge and link that to what you want to teach them. Suppose you want to improve defending and, more concretely, improve your players' posture in a duel while defending. You could do it in this following manner:

"Guys, what's the most important thing to defend?"

"The goal, of course."

"That's right. What can you do to defend the goal?"

I get answers like 'take the ball' and 'go stand between the goal and the opponent.'

"That's right," I say, "and you have another important instrument, your posture. We're going to practice that in a duel. Position yourself between your own goal and the opponent with the ball and force the player to the outside with your posture." I may show it first with a player so the team knows exactly what I'm talking about. However, the best thing is when a player gives the example.

- *Align with what your players already know, and then they learn something new more easily.*

Playing Principles

There are coaches who organise their way of play with playing principles. You can compare a playing principle with a value within an organization. Such a value directs everyone in that organization on what to do in different situations. For example, if a value is 'honesty,' then you are honest with the other person, even if the truth is not pretty or nice. It is a compass. Such a value is called a playing principle in soccer.

A well-known principle in soccer is the five-second rule; if your team loses the ball to the opponent, the nearest two to three players press the opponent within five seconds. The purpose is to avoid a dangerous counterattack. Another goal is to recover the ball as quickly as possible. No matter where on the pitch, at what minute of the game, or how tired the players are, the five-second rule is the principle that guides every player's behavior. When the ball is lost up front, the closest players put pressure on, often that's the strikers. If there is a loss of ball in midfield, the midfielders will probably come into action. This game principle is reflected in teams of Guardiola, Klopp, Bosz, Schmidt, and Ten Hag, for example.

Coaches use game principles for several reasons. One reason is that in soccer, there are a lot of different situations that you can't all train. The playing principles then offer a foothold for the players. Another reason is that a playing principle gives players autonomy. They decide themselves how to solve the situation because a principle offers several possibilities. These principles give them clarity on what to do and feed into their feeling of competence. Players become independent and creative in playing. Another advantage of playing principles is that they apply to every player on the team. This increases team cohesiveness. Moreover, playing principles allow players to coach each other. Every player can come up with solutions and help his teammates with them. The big challenge with playing principles lies in the application. Do your players understand them? And can they apply the principles during a match? It's on you whether you want to work with playing principles.

- *Playing principles direct players to find and invent their own solutions. That makes players creative and independent and increases team cohesiveness.*

Formations and Fixed Patterns

There are also coaches who train from fixed formations with fixed patterns with which they provide coherence. This is the more traditional way of playing.

A formation is a basic arrangement of how the players position themselves on the pitch. For example, 1-4-4-2 means that a team plays with a goalkeeper, four defenders, four midfielders, and two attackers. Several types of formations are possible. With those formations, training is being done, and players get to handle what they can do. Handle in the sense of understanding of and acting on formations and patterns. For example, if our backs go higher, then our defensive midfielder slumps between the central defenders. These patterns are trained so that during the match, the players are able to carry out the plan. The big advantage is that formations with patterns provide players with a lot of direction during the match which fuels their feeling of competence. The big downside is that opponents can recognize the patterns and come up with solutions to overcome them. What do your players do when the trained pattern is thwarted during the match? Are they then able to switch to a different pattern, or can they come up with a totally different solution? If they can not and don't know what to do, then you risk your players losing their feeling of competence.

- *Formations give players a lot of grip on their position on the pitch and the execution of a plan. The disadvantage is that formations do not provide solutions to unexpected situations.*

Provide a Shared Mental Model

Playing principles, formations, and fixed patterns contribute to the shared mental model of your players. A shared mental model means that everyone on the team knows what the idea or plan is. You can also make the literal coherence between your players clear, whether you choose playing principles or formations with patterns as a starting point. Suppose you want to build up, but every time your centre-back has the ball, your attackers move towards the ball, and they make the playing field smaller. That's why you think of an exercise to improve the cohesion of your players and their shared mental model in building up.

In the explanation of the exercise, you tell what the players already know, "We want to make the playing field as big as possible when we have the ball because then we have more time and space to play."

Then you do the exercise and let the players experience. Again the strikers move towards the ball when the ball is with the central defender. Now you go get started with the 'shared mental model' of your players. You make sure that every player understands what a large playing field looks like when the centre-back has the ball.

"Okay, guys. What do our attackers do when the ball is at the feet of our centre-back?"

Often there is at least one player who has it in mind and says, "Our attackers all move towards the ball."

To which I reply, "Exactly, that's what I see too. We want the playing field to be as big as possible. Does that happen when the attackers all move towards the ball?"

"No, then we'll make it smaller."

"Indeed. And that makes it difficult for us. What can the attackers do?"

Basically, there are two options that the players can come up with. Either the attackers keep their position, often the simplest solution. The alternative is that the moves of the attackers are tuned with that of the midfielders. A striker moves towards the ball, and a midfielder makes a run to the attacker's position. This is working on your players 'shared mental model.' They know they have to make the playing field as big as possible in attack, and with this exercise and explanation, it becomes clear to them what that looks like. This way, you can also work on the 'shared mental model' in the defense and transition phases. Actually, you attune with each other so that you all start to speak the same language. Everyone on the team knows what is meant by certain words and plans.

A great advantage of speaking the same language and having the same mental model as a team is that everyone can coach each other because every player knows what the goal is.

Of course, players also dare open their mouths. In this lies a role for you as a coach. You ensure the establishment and monitoring of the team culture. But, in my experience, knowing what the agreements are is the most important factor in teaching your players to coach each other.

- *A shared mental model means that all players have the same image of what, for example, a playing principle means and what that looks like on the pitch. As a result, everyone speaks the same language, and players can coach each other. This provides intrinsic motivation and a belief in your own abilities.*

Let Players Experience Why an Exercise Is Important

An important insight for coaches is that most people overestimate their own qualities, the so-called Dunning-Kruger effect. Chances are one or more of your players also overestimate themselves and are unconsciously incompetent. That's not what you want because it can hinder your players' intrinsic motivation to train. Why would a player who believes he has mastered something already still want to train on that? You just want your players to realize they can still improve themselves so that they are open to training.

The best way to make your players aware of this is to have them experience so. Arrange a friendly match against a better opponent in which the points for improvement become clear to your players. Or, during training, bring your players into a type of situation they have difficulty with. They experience they are not yet able to achieve the goal or do so with a lot of difficulties. Then you start asking questions and sharing your observations. This is how you make players aware of the steps they can still take. Then you do exercises to work on those specific skills. You close with the first situation to see if your players have progressed. This is how you make the alignment clear between their skills and the reason for your exercises. That works motivating for your players, especially if they are not really excited about a particular exercise. Most players don't like fitness training, for example. But if you show them the alignment between fitness training and their goals, it motivates them to do their best.

> • *What you want to achieve is that your players see the alignment between what they do in matches and what you train with them. Letting your players experience is the strongest way and leads to insight and*

understanding. The better they understand how to work as a team and the better their understanding of the training goals and coherence, the better they will perform and develop.

Summary

How do you make sure your players understand why you train the way you train?

Your players can apply in a match what they have learned during training when they understand the coherence.

Using playing principles or formations can help.

Most important is establishing coherence by aligning what players already know and can do, that you work on a shared mental model and that players experience why an exercise is needed.

6.3 How Do You Train As Holistically As Possible?

"I am building a fire, and every day I train, I add more fuel."

- Mia Hamm

The training goal and how you can align with your players are clear. Which training strategy do you use? In football, everything is interconnected. Tactics, technique, physical, and social-emotional are at any time connected to one another. A player can perform in the first three areas if he is socially-emotional stable. A strong fear of failure affects tactical, technical, and physical performance. In addition, attacking and defending are linked. You can't attack in a match without the risk of having to transition and defend. And vice versa, when you defend, you can get opportunities to attack.

Therefore, train as holistically as possible, or soccer real. Do as many exercises as possible in which both attacking, transitions and defending as tactical, technical, physical, and social-emotional skills are featured so that the translation from training to the match is easier for your players. Then you also address them on their intrinsic motivation and increase their belief in their own abilities.

Do you find it difficult to design exercises in which both attacking as transitioning and defending are included? Play small-sided games or mini-matches. Utilize your chosen goals with skills and/or principles, then determine what you pay attention to and how you coach your players during the game.

Games can be 1v1, 2v2, 3v3, through 11v11. But you can also, given your number of players, play with under- or overload 3v2, 4v3, 5v4 or with jokers 2v2+1, 4v4+2, 8v8+3.

Dry Training versus Competitive Training

There is a lot of discussion among coaches about 'dry training' versus 'competitive training.' Some coaches swear by dry exercises without resistance. Because with these kinds of exercises, they can improve the technique of their players. In my view, that statement is correct. For me, the definition of dry training is 'training the motor execution of a football technique.' The big disadvantage, the reason why I'm not such a big fan of dry training, is that it has little connection with the game of soccer. It is a little realistic. In a match, a player must recognize the football situation, make the best or most creative choice and execute it motorically. With dry exercises, you train one aspect, the motor execution, but you miss the coherence with the other aspects. An unambiguous answer in this discussion is something I don't have, and honesty compels me to say that I also do a dry exercise every now and then.

Johan Cruijff was also not a fan of dry exercises. He was a fan of learning soccer through play. You learn to play soccer by playing soccer, like in the streets, not through contrived exercises with pawns. "Have you ever seen a player on the streets collide with a lamppost? No, because every player scans before making an action. How many players on the streets go down during a game? Not many because they know the stones are hard. (...) So players in the streets, first of all, learn to look at opponents and obstacles before making a move." Learning soccer through play is the best teacher Cruijff thought because that resembles soccer best. The chaos and unpredictability you experience during soccer are not there in dry exercises.

I recommend doing dry exercises only if your players are not yet able to execute a technique motor-wise. A player who can't pass a ball with his laces yet has to first practice it in a dry way without resistance so that he can master that technique. From the moment he has learned to do so, incorporate this technique in a training exercise with resistance or in a game. Then he can learn to pass the ball over a larger distance under pressure at the right time, in the right direction, and at the right speed because he should be able to do that in a match.

A player who wants to get started on his own, in principle, only needs a ball and a wall to train his motor technique.

> • *Only use a dry exercise whenever a player hasn't mastered the motor execution of a technical skill. Whenever the player has mastered it, expose him to a training exercise with resistance or a game.*

Playing Under Pressure

Finally, your players may experience pressure playing a match. You want to prepare them as well as possible during training. But can you replicate the pressure of the match in a training session? According to Teun Koopmeiners, who was a regular penalty taker at AZ and now plays with Italian side Atalanta Bergamo, you can. I don't believe you can mimic the exact situation or match pressure. You can only experience what something is like when you actually do it. But, I do believe that you can prepare for it. You can train under pressure with your players, so they can deal with pressure during the match better. In my third season at PSV, almost every U9-U12 team won its penalty series during tournaments. That was no coincidence because in that season, we started training on taking penalties under pressure with those teams.

In *Top Dog: the science of winning and losing* Po Bronson and Ashley Merryman write the way one appraises a competitive situation has a big effect on the functioning of the brain and body.

Thus, mindset makes a big difference. Viewing competition as a challenge, as opposed to a threat, switches on a different brain system and with that, affects the way the body functions, leading to a more effective oxygen circulation for example. Mindset influences performance. Your players' mindset on this is interesting to discover to help them deal with pressure better. Anson Dorrance has been quite successful as a women's soccer coach at the University of North Carolina. In 30 years, he won twenty-one championships with his teams. His take on pressure? Train under pressure as preparation for the match, but lower pressure around and during matches.

How do you train under pressure? For example, during a small-sided game, two teams play against each other. A team earns a penalty per goal scored. At the end of the game, the score reflects the number of penalties to be taken. For example, the final score is 4-3 for team A. The team has not won yet, because the penalty shootout determines which team wins. Team A takes four penalties because they have scored four goals. Team B gets to take three penalties. The team that scores the most penalties wins. Both teams are on the center line, and the penalty taker runs from the center line to the penalty spot. I can tell you from experience that there is pressure, and players also like it.

You can think of many more exercises under pressure. Keep in mind there should always be something at stake that your players want to achieve. The keep-up challenge, as described in chapter 3.1, is an example thereof; the consequence that players who failed the challenge were not allowed to train caused the pressure.

How do you help a player who struggles with pressure? Training under pressure initially leads to awareness. What happens to a player under pressure? What does he do? What does he think? What does he say? What does he feel? Whatever it is, it's okay, and there are always solutions. In chapter 6.2, you can read more about this. Get started with the player by, for example, setting goals; see the video 'Chapter 3.2: Setting goals'. Let a player visualize that he succeeds; see the video 'Chapter 6.3: Visualizing'. Or, do a breathing exercise; see the video 'Chapter 3.2: Breathing exercise.'

Watch the videos via the links on: https://www.bauer-vandelooij.nl/bijlage-boek.

- *Training under pressure provides insights into and about your players. Observe well what happens to your players under pressure and help them in dealing with that pressure. This leads to a stronger belief in one's own abilities and better performance during times of pressure, such as in competitions.*

Learning Strategies

During training, your players act continuously towards a goal, such as playing better passes, winning more duels, scoring a goal, preventing the opponent from scoring a goal, keeping the ball in the team, recovering the ball, outplaying an opponent, making a save, you name it. Multiple strategies can work to achieve the same goal. For example, you can score a goal with a shot from a distance, with a header, or from a rebound. The strategy a player uses is important in achieving the goal because not every strategy is equally successful. The more strategies a player masters, the greater the chance he will act on his goal and improve his performance. Focus on your individual coaching on those strategies. It turns out that feedback on metacognitive and process levels is most effective. What is that? That is questioning the player about what he wants to achieve, what he saw and thought, what and why he did what he did, and what he could do differently next time. The player shares his observations and choice, his strategy, with you. You can get started with that. If the player improves his strategy, then he is more likely to achieve his goal.

Some examples:

"I saw my teammate in a free space standing twenty meters away and wanted to pass the ball to him."

"How did you pass the ball?"

"With the inside."

"Did the ball arrive?"

"No."

"How can you pass that ball so that your teammates receive the ball next time?"

"With my laces."

"I would like to dribble."

"Okay, how do you practice that?"

"No idea."

"Name a player who is very good at dribbling."

"Neymar."

"Okay, what is that he does?"

"I don't know. I'll have to go see videos of him for that."

"Sounds like a plan."

"I put pressure on the player with the ball."

"So what happened?"

"He gave a through ball to a man in my back."

"Too bad. What did you see that made you move out?"

"I saw him standing free and thought I had to get there right away so he couldn't shoot."

"Okay. Did you also see what kind of space you gave away as a result?"

"No."

"What can you do in the following situation to decide whether to move out or not?"

"First, see where the other central defender is or communicate with him."

"I had forgotten my football shorts and socks, and that's why I wasn't allowed to play."

"That's a shame. Who packed your bag?"

"I did."

"When did you do that?"

"Early this morning, quite rushed."

"Is it more common for you to forget something when you're in a hurry?"

"Yeah, not very often, but sometimes."

"Okay, what can you learn from that?"

"Maybe packing when I'm not in a rush."

"Give an example. When is a good time to pack your bag?"

"Maybe the night before."

- *Asking questions leads to a greater learning effect and also stimulates your player's intrinsic motivation and belief in his own abilities.*

The Feedback Cycle

A model you can use in giving effective feedback might be Hattie and Timperley's Feedback Cycle. It consists of three phases.

First phase is Feed Up. Here you establish your player's goal. Where is he going to? This is very important as this goal directs your feedback. Establish your player's goal: What were you aiming for? This makes him think (again) on what he's going for. Plus you can see what he already knows.

Second phase is Feedback. How is he going? Here you share how he is going in your opinion. Use your observations to tell your player to what extent he's achieved his goal.

Third and last phase is Feedforward. Where to next? Here you tell your player what he can do to reach his goal next time. Keep doing x and if you add this or that, then your chances of reaching your goal will be greater.

It works very well to have your player go through these steps as well.

An example from my experience as teacher in Applied Psychology. A student wants feedback on his problem analysis.

'You want my feedback on your analysis. What in your opinion are features of a good analysis? To what extent does your current analysis meets those features in your opinion? Ask one or two other students for their opinion too. Once you've done this, you can come back to me to ask me specific questions. In the meantime I will read you analysis and judge it based upon your criteria. So we can compare our judgements.'

This makes him think (again) on his goal and what's needed to achieve it. Plus he also gets feedback from others but most importantly from himself as well. I'd like him to learn to do this reflection himself and use other people, like me, as a second opinion. In the feedback phase I tend to compare my student's feedback with my feedback to see where we agree and where we differ. This gives both of us insight my student's thinking process. I like to do this especially because him and I are calibrating on those criteria and hopefully he gets to establish more and more what is needed to meet the criteria himself. So he has more direction next times. In the feedforward phase my favorite question is: 'What is your next step(s)?' However it depends on the student whether I start or end with this question. I'd rather start with, especially when I think the student understands what he's doing. But sometimes I reckon it's more effective to first tell what steps I'd recommend. Then asking my favorite question comes last and serves as a check to see if the student can get on and with what.

One of the biggest advantages of this model to me is that you get to align to your player's or student's goal so that you're on the same page. And that it's focus is explicit on the work instead of the person. In my experience players and students become very open to feedback. Why is this? It feels as if establishing the goal takes out all thoughts or perceptions of my student or player doubting my reasons for giving him feedback. For example, chances of him thinking that I don't like him and therefore give him feedback that it's not yet good enough become slimmer. Because he experiences it's all about his goal and whether or not he's reached it. If he hasn't reached it, he gets me helping him to get there next time. It works the same in coaching your players on actions in attacking, defending, or transitioning.

Summary

Train as holistically as possible. That resembles a soccer match best.

Do as many exercises as possible in which players have to both attack and defend in which tactical, technical, physical, and socio-emotional components are featured.

Teach players to handle pressure.

Ask players about their observations and choices or their strategies. Get started with them.

6.4 How Can You Convey Skills, Attitude, And Knowledge?

"The athletes who improved the most in sports performance were the athletes who came to train most often."

- Steve Magness

Many coaches I have mentored doubted their skills as a coach. These coaches indeed had trouble giving training, but that had not so much to do with a lack of fun exercises or enthusiasm. More often, it had to do with the lack of frames or rules of conduct within which players can behave.

Clear Frames

A lack of a clear framework can lead to chaos, and that makes it difficult for every coach to give good and fun training.

An example of a team without clear frameworks. At the start of the training, some players are not yet present, and the question is whether and at what time they will come if they do. This can cause chaos from the beginning. When the coach speaks, players hardly listen. They are still playing or talking to each other. It sometimes looks like a traffic situation with the coach as a traffic cop.

You obviously don't want to experience this scenario. Give your players a clear frame and spend time around a training session at the beginning of the season to determine such a framework and standards and values. Read chapter 5.2, 'Team agreements,' again on how to deal with that. If there's no other way, you even do it in instead of a training session. Believe me, you'll benefit from it the entire season. Clear frameworks are a precondition for training and provide peace of mind and focus.

If the frameworks are in place, you can give training. Training is all about transferring skills, attitudes, and knowledge. In that, you, as a coach, need didactic skills. Didactics means the art of teaching. I have experienced that three didactic principles help in giving good training in terms of discipline, clarity, and necessity.

• Clear frames are a prerequisite for a training and ensure focus and calm.

Discipline

Discipline is the first didactic principle for giving soccer practice. By discipline, I mean 'acting according to ambition and acting towards the goal.' Your players have ambitions and goals as an individual and as a team. You see to it that your players act accordingly. Keeping promises and agreements is also part of this, both on and off the pitch. In chapter 2.4, I have given an extensive example of this under the heading 'Create a we-feeling.'

The consequence of discipline in the team is that you, your staff, and your players learn that you can rely on each other. The great thing about discipline is that it becomes a habit over time and does not require extra energy.

What can be difficult about discipline is that sometimes you get in conflict with your players because you see to it that they comply with the agreements, and there are consequences if they don't. I can't say it often enough, you determine, with your behavior, what the agreement is worth. If you tolerate a player who does not comply with an agreement, you give a signal to all players that the appointment is worth little. This costs you reliability. It's even worse if you do hold certain players to those agreements but not others. With that, you don't just throw your reliability but also undermine the team's cohesiveness and your players' respect for you.

> • *Make agreements you think are important enough to get into a conflict over with every player on your team, and be consistent in acting on those agreements. That reinforces discipline and team cohesiveness.*

Clarity

Clarity is the second didactic principle. Does the player understand what you expect from him during an exercise? You have what you want to train all in your head. It is up to you to explain the exercise so that each player, preferably immediately, understands.

What can help you with your explanation is talk, picture, and act. You tell what the intention is, set an example for players to watch, and let your players do it once. Our brains have a verbal and non-verbal processing system. If both systems are addressed, you process the information better. The explanation of an exercise is important but not necessarily very fun for players. Therefore, keep the explanation as short and concise as possible. For example, only tell the goal and the rules of the game. Thereafter you can play for a short period of time to let the players practice so that you see that they have understood. Of course, you can also check with your players whether they have understood you by asking, 'Was my explanation clear?'

> • *Use the principle of 'talk, picture, act' when you explain the exercise. That appeals to the brain so that your players understand the exercise better.*

Need

Adding necessity to the exercise is the third step within your didactics for a good soccer training session. There's always a necessity in a match, because the opponent also wants to win the match and so will do their very best. If handling, passing or dribbling with the ball is not good, the ball is more likely to be taken. With training, you prepare your players as best as possible for the matches. How do you create that same need in training as in a match?

By designing the exercise in such a way that a player cannot act in another way. This is called implicit training.

Do you want to improve your dribbling? Play a game where your players can score a point by dribbling through gates of pawns or over lines. You don't have to tell them to dribble (explicit coaching). The exercise forces them to do so. Do you want your players to be faster in ball handling? Make the dimensions of the playing field smaller so that they have less space and, therefore, less time. The practice is the master and forces your players to behave, and you help them to improve that behavior. What often works as well is adding a game element to the exercises. Players compete against each other or against themselves. As you have read in chapter 2.3, under the heading 'Changing motivation,' I prefer to compete against self because that's the best measure for development.

CH#6 - Training

Johan Cruijff has a similar view on the necessity of training. As a coach, you can increase resistance.

"For example, to make them better, don't force them to stop dribbling. Instead of putting two older guys down, make it three or four. If they then have dribbled past two opponents, the third kicks them. Make it as difficult as possible. In practice, the player experiences what works and what doesn't. That's a better lesson than you telling your players," Cruijff said.

By adding necessity to the exercise, you shift your role somewhat as a coach. Chances are your players are even more open to your tips and feedback because they want to achieve their goals, and you can help them with that. You become more the coach who guides and supports his players. That is also a nice (learn) experience for work. According to Harvard Business Review, business leadership is shifting increasingly from listening to questioning, and guiding team members.

- *The necessity in an exercise increases intrinsic motivation, creativity, maximum effort, and the collaborative ability of your players.*

The Coach Makes the Difference

Summary

Conveying skills, attitude, and knowledge by setting clear frameworks and using didactic principles:

Discipline.

Clarity.

Need.

6.5 What Are Good Soccer Exercises

"Good training is priceless."

- Lailah Gifty Akita

Good soccer practice improves your players' individual and team performances. In good soccer practice, intrinsic motivation, belief in your own abilities, culture, didactic principles, and soccer content come together. Because so many things come together, it is and remains for every coach at every level challenging to design good soccer exercises.

Think from big to small in designing your training sessions and exercises. What is the way of play? How's that ensured in the training sessions and exercises? How do you align with what your players already know and can do? Then determine which principle, pattern and/or skill you specifically want to train so that you and your players can focus on that.

Improving your players' performance is more effective when they are intrinsically motivated. Therefore let your players make their own choices within the exercise. Think of goals, for example, in scoring, with which your players can experience success quickly and often. Make sure players work together, which stimulates connectedness.

In a good exercise, your players experience what works and what doesn't. Make them aware of their influence. What can they do to achieve the training goal? That stimulates their belief in their own ability. In addition, you may discover the beliefs of your players with which you can or need to work. It's strong when practice, and not you, forces your players to show the behaviors you want to train. This is possible with necessity in the exercise, such as a game element, making the exercise the master. Make sure you have a clear explanation of the exercise so that your players understand.

What players learn in training should match the game. The learning transfer is important. Does the exercise resemble what players experience during the match? The more the exercise resembles the match, the more powerful the learning transfer will be. Basically, 11v11 is the best soccer practice to get better in the match, given it's 11v11. Due to the physical health of your players and the chance that some players won't be involved for minutes in the game, you don't play 11v11 continuously but do your exercises in smaller numbers. In this, players become more active, and basically, there are more repetitions. This makes your role more important; how does the exercise relate to the playing style during the match? In your explanation and coaching, align with what your players can and know. The power of a good training session has not only got to do with good exercises but certainly also with the relationship between those exercises within the session. They have a common focus that returns in the different exercises of that session.

Your coaching during training is a tool for your players to perform better. In coaching, I mainly ask questions so that my players start to think and become even more involved in the exercise. In doing so, I respond to their intrinsic motivation and belief in their own abilities. We also work on their shared mental model. How do they work together towards the goal? This leads to better mutual understanding, communication, and collaboration. Finally, we link it to the match so the learning transfer is increased.

The questions I ask are roughly related to what the player wants to achieve, what the player sees or recognizes, and what plan or solution the player can come up with. They are mostly open and non-directive questions. How do you do that? If your question starts with what, where, who, when, or how, you're often on the right track.

Some general examples of these questions: What is the goal? What are you and your team doing to achieve the goal? What does the opposing team do? Where on the field does it take place? Who are involved? When will that happen? How can you solve that? What can you and your team do differently to achieve the goal? How does this resemble what happens in the match?

Finally, it may happen that the exercise does not go exactly as you wish. What do you do then? What do you want to see in your players when things in the match are not running smoothly? Do you want them to come up with excuses, or do you want them to own the situation? That answer determines your actions because you lead by example with your behaviour. You can use the following checklist use so that every exercise helps your players become better soccer players.

Checklist:

✓ Intrinsic motivation.

Does the exercise stimulate your players' intrinsic motivation? Can your players make their own choices? Does the exercise provides experiences of success, and does the exercise ensures collaboration and connectedness?

✓ Belief in one's own abilities.

The Coach Makes the Difference

Do your players experience what they can do to increase their chances of success?

✓ Clarity/discipline/necessity.

Do your players understand the exercise? Does the exercise have a necessity that implicitly forces players to show the behaviors you want to train?

✓ Learning transfer.

Does the exercise resemble what your players experience in the match?

✓ Your coaching.

Do you explain the exercise clearly? Does your explanation align with what the player already knows and can do? Do you contribute with your coaching to their intrinsic motivation, belief in their own abilities, the shared mental model, and the learning transfer?

• *The coherence between exercises and the match is important. Along with asking open and non-directive questions, your players learn more effectively. It also leads to more intrinsic motivation, a stronger belief in their own abilities, and better performance during the match.*

Example of what can go wrong:

Four players stand in a square, one at each corner point. They pass the ball around to each other clockwise. The goal is to improve technique.

CH#6 - Training

Example 1 of what could go wrong

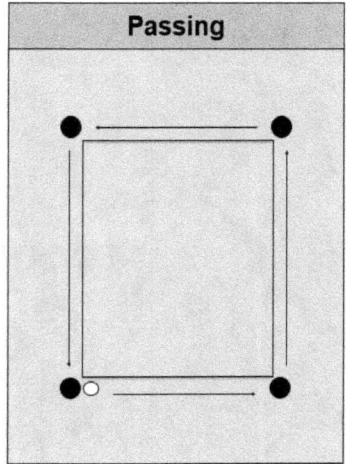

Intrinsic motivation: Players are not making their own choices but are only executing motor behavior. It can be challenging at the start, but the feeling of competence fades quite fast, and there is limited connection.

Belief in one's own abilities: Players quickly experience what works and what doesn't.

Clarity/discipline/necessity: Exercise is easy to understand, but necessity is lacking.

Learning transfer: Not holistic, not appealing to all skills.

Your coaching: If you want your players to continue to give their best, you must coach and instruct them a lot and forcefully. The danger? They give their best only because you say so.

Chances are your players will give their best in the first three to five minutes because it is a new situation. But the exercise isn't strong on intrinsic motivation. It quickly makes it clear to players what works and what doesn't, although they probably already know that, given the simplicity of the exercise. A necessity and a learning transfer are missing, so the danger lurks that your players will improve little, and you extrinsically motivate your players with your coaching.

How then?

3v1

Example of what you could do

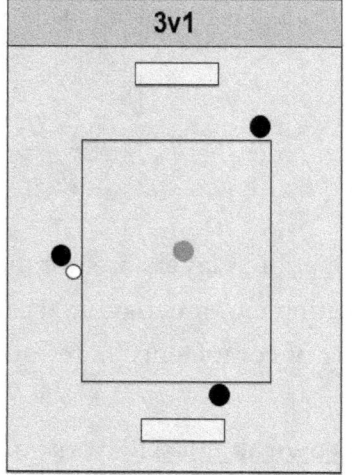

In the same square, with a small goal on two sides, a 3v1 rondo is being played. The exercise has a game element and, therefore, a necessity so that the player does his best. In addition, players can make their own choices in this game. The three players in a team earn a point per ten seconds for possession of the ball. The defender earns three points if he intercepts the ball and scores in one of the two goals. These ways of scoring offer fast and often experiences of success and force the player to persevere after an error or failed action.

Intrinsic motivation: Players make their own choices and experience success quickly, and often, the three players have to work together, which creates a bond.

Belief in your own abilities: Players quickly experience what works and what doesn't.

Clarity/discipline/necessity: Exercise is simple to understand, with a need.

Learning transfer: Holistic, appeals to all skills.

Your coaching: You can coach players on technique.

In the example below, I give an improved version of the pass-and-kick exercise in which the aim is to give each other feedback and stimulate a growth mindset.

In a square, four players stand at each corner. Every time the ball has gone around, the team earns a point. They play five rounds of one minute each.

Goal: To pass the ball around as many times as possible. The goal in the first round is to score as many points as possible. The goal in the next rounds is to improve the previous score. With this game element, there is an explicit necessity in the excercise. Because something is at stake, the connection becomes important. In addition, the development becomes visible because the players probably improve their number of points. Between rounds, you can encourage players to give each other feedback; what is your teammate already doing well, and what could he do better? The big disadvantage remains that the exercise is not holistic. It also does not give your players the freedom to make their own choices.

Intrinsic motivation: Players do not make their own choices but execute and experience success quickly, and often, it appeals to the connection.

The Coach Makes the Difference
Example 2 of what could go wrong

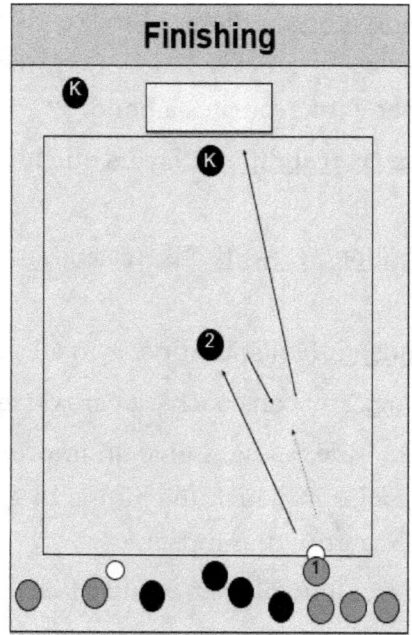

<u>Believe in one's own abilities:</u> Players quickly experience what works and what doesn't.

<u>Clarity/discipline/necessity:</u> Exercise is simple to understand, with a need.

<u>Learning transfer:</u> Not holistic, not appealing to all skills.

<u>Your coaching:</u> You can encourage players to give each other feedback and focus on a growth mindset.

Another example of what can go wrong.

You do a finishing exercise around the box to improve your finishing and scoring goals. Player one makes a one-two with player two and then shoots at the goal. Player one takes the place of player two, and player two retrieves the ball and lines up in the back of the queue, where eight players are still standing to wait.

The two goalkeepers defend two balls and then switch with each other.

<u>Intrinsic motivation:</u> Players make somewhat their own choices but are mainly executing, challenging at first, but the feeling of competence fades quickly, and there is limited connection.

<u>Believe in one's own abilities</u>: Players quickly experience what works and what doesn't.

<u>Clarity/discipline/necessity:</u> Practice is simple to understand, but it lacks a necessity. Waiting in a row for your turn provides room for distractions and unwanted behavior.

<u>Learning transfer:</u> Not holistic, not appealing to all skills.

<u>Your coaching:</u> If you want your players to continue to give their best, you must coach them a lot. The danger? They have to do their best because you say so.

How then?

The Coach Makes the Difference

1+kv1+k

Example of what you could do

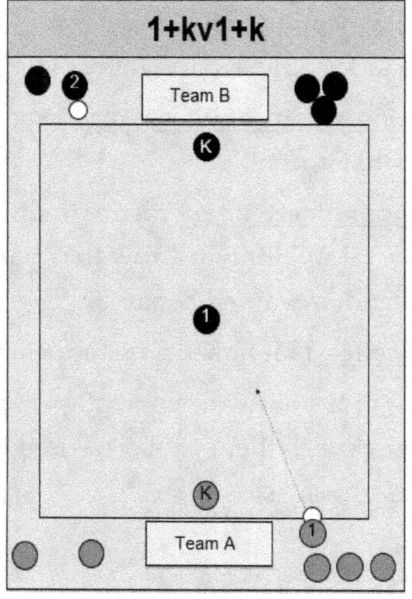

Two teams play against each other through 1v1 duels with goalkeepers. The exercise has a game element and is thus a necessity so that the player does his best. Player one of team A dribbles into the pitch and duels with player one of team B. Does the ball go in the goal or out of play? Then dribbles a third player with the ball into the pitch, in this case, player two from team B for a new 1v1. Player one of team A stays on the pitch and transitions to defending, and Player one from Team B leaves the pitch. This forces the player from team A to continue after a goal or failed action because the next duel is already upcoming. Again, the ball goes in the goal or out of play? Then player two of team A dribbles into the pitch, player one of Team A leaves the pitch, and player two of Team B transitions into defending. The goalkeepers are continuously challenged to stay focused and participate. So it goes on for six minutes. The team that scored the most goals in those six minutes wins the round. This exercise is holistic and appeals to all skills. The exercise resembles a match situation.

<u>Intrinsic motivation:</u> Players can make their own choices in achieving the goal, quick success experiences, and have connectedness within the team.

<u>Belief in one's own abilities:</u> Players experience what doesn't, but also what does work, thanks to your coaching. You can also discover their beliefs and work on them.

<u>Necessity/discipline/clarity:</u> Exercise is simple to understand, with a need.

<u>Learning transfer:</u>   Holistic, all skills involved.

<u>Your coaching:</u> You can coach players in their way of finishing/scoring.

Practice 1: 4v4+4

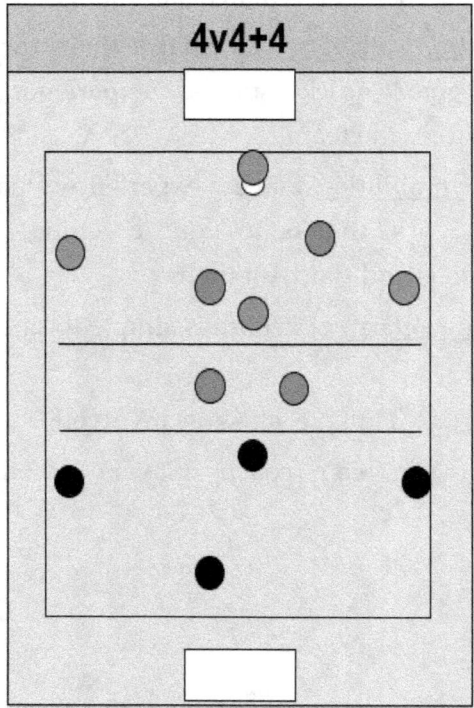

Practice 1

A rectangle, with a small goal on each side, is divided into two compartments with a center strip.

Three teams of four play against each other. Two teams work together and are the attacking teams against the third team that defends. There is a game element that forces the players to do their best. The attacking teams are positioned both in one of two compartments, for example, team A on one end and team B on the other. The defensive team C has two players in the box where the ball is and two players in the center strip. The attacking teams earn a point if they pass the ball from their box to the team at the other end. This looks like a match situation where a team builds up and is pressured by the other team. When the defending team intercepts the ball then they can score in the goal adjacent to the box of or pass the ball to the team in the other box for a point. This resembles a match situation after recovery. The player who recovered the ball has a choice, does he seek the space forward, or does he keep the ball? The ways of earning points create a sense of competence and belief in one's own abilities because points can be earned quickly. The attacking team that has lost the ball becomes the defending team. A team that loses the ball can't get hung up on that because the opponents continue to play for points to earn. Does the ball go out of play? Then the team that played the ball out of play becomes the defending team. This exercise is holistic and appeals to all skills.

With the training goals you have chosen and your explanation of the exercise, you provide clarity to the players. Tell them how the exercise fits within the principles or patterns of the way you play so that you also align with what your players already know and can do. With your coaching during the exercise, you stimulate your players' shared mental model, and their belief in their own abilities, and you can discover and change their beliefs.

<u>Intrinsic motivation:</u> Players can make their own choices in achieving the goal, have quick experiences of success, and there's connectedness within the team(s).

<u>Belief in one's own abilities</u>: Players experience what doesn't, but also what does work, thanks to your coaching. You can also discover their beliefs and work on them with your coaching.

<u>Necessity/discipline/clarity:</u> Players need some time to understand the exercise. There's a necessity.

<u>Learning transfer:</u> Holistic. All skills strengthen with your explanation and coaching.

The Coach Makes the Difference

Your coaching: What is the goal? Outplay the opponents by passing the ball to the team in the other box. What do you pay attention to? Whether there is space between the defenders to pass the ball to the other box. Be open with your body posture so that you can see the ball, your teammates, the opponents, and the other box as much as possible. When does that space between defenders emerge? By changing sides at a high pace and/or when defenders get tired. Who in the other box do you prefer to play the ball to and why? The one furthest away because he has the most time and space before defenders can put pressure on him. What will your plan be? Create space between defenders to pass the ball through by either switching sides at high speed and then searching for the farthest man or by keeping possession, tiring opponents and waiting for the space to emerge, and then looking for the furthest man with a pass.

Do you recognize the connection between this exercise and the match? Yes, it resembles building up, but also how to defend and put pressure.

Practice 2: 4v2 -> 4v6

Practice 2

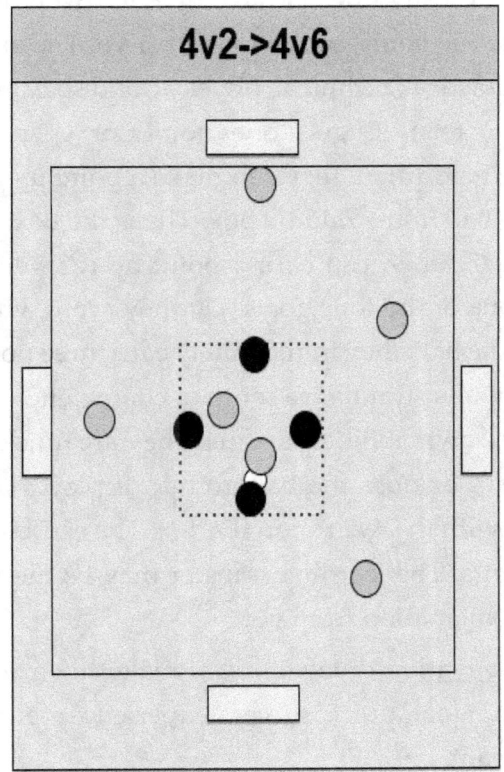

Two teams play against each other, team A with four players and team B with six players. There is a game element that gives the players the need to do their best. The game consists of two parts. The game starts with part one, in which Team A is playing a 4v2 rondo against two players of team B. Because there is something at stake, the player becomes forced into bonding with his team. Team A wins a point per 10 seconds that they have possession. Does team B recover the ball, or does the ball go out of the 4v2 box? Then starts a 6v4 for team B in a larger playing field (part 2). These two parts provide a certain chaos that challenges players to be fully focused and disciplined while playing soccer. The player who loses the ball in part one basically doesn't have time to dwell on that for a long time because the game goes on in part two. The exercise is holistic and calls on tactical, technical, physical, and social-emotional skills. In part two, team B gets one point for every 20 seconds of possession. In addition, they can make a point by getting someone to touch the ball in the middle box. That's the box in which the 4v2 was played. Team A can earn a point by recovering the ball and scoring in one of the four goals. Do they score within ten seconds of winning the ball, they immediately earn three points. These ways of earning points stimulate a sense of competence, and the belief in your players' own abilities, because they are quickly achievable. Is a goal scored, or does the ball go out of play? Then the exercise starts again with the 4v2 rondo (Part 1). The exercise contains many positive points. The learning transfer may be the least good point and needs explanation from you.

Intrinsic motivation: players can make their own choices in achieving the goal, quick success experiences, and connectedness within the team.

Belief in one's own abilities: Players experience what doesn't, but also what does work, thanks to your coaching. You can also discover your players' beliefs and work on them.

Necessity/discipline/clarity: Players need some time to understand the exercise. There's a necessity.

Learning transfer: Holistic, all skills, but your explanation and coaching are important.

Your coaching (focused on the switch a->v): What is the goal after you lose the ball in the 4v2? The direct pressure on the opponent with the ball. What does that mean? That the opponent does not pass between us, and we immediately recover the ball. Who does what after losing the ball? The nearest two players at the ball put pressure. The other two players make it compact. What if you fail to win the ball back immediately? Then we group ourselves and make sure that the ball cannot be passed between us. We keep the ball on one side, and if we're in the right position, we're going to put pressure. When is a good time to press? First, we have to be compact around the opponent with the ball and put pressure on a bad pass, bad handling of the ball, or in a situation where a player receives the ball but is face-down. Do you recognize the connection between this exercise and the match? Yes, basically anywhere on the field, you can lose or win the ball.

Practice 3: 8v8+1

Practice 3

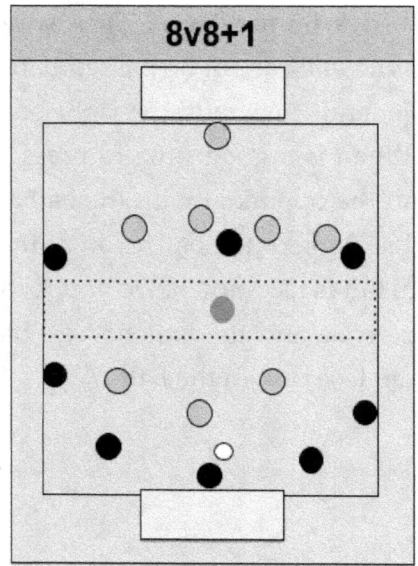

A rectangle, with a big goal on both ends, is divided into two boxes with a center strip. Two teams of eight players play against each other with one joker.

There is a game element that gives the players the need to do their best. On your own half, it is 4+kv3. On the opponent's half, it is 3v4+k, and the joker is in the middle section. In attack, one player crosses into the opponent's half. Then it becomes 4+jokerv4+k on the half of the top and 3+kv3 in their own half.

A team has to score at the opponent's half and gets there by dribbling through the strip or via a one-two pass with the joker. This exercise is holistic, calls on all skills, and is played on areas of the pitch resembling a match which makes it much like 11v11, and therefore a strong learning transfer exists.

<u>Intrinsic motivation:</u> Players can make their own choices in achieving the goal, slower but match-like success experiences, and connectedness within the team.

<u>Belief in one's own abilities:</u> Players experience what doesn't, but also what does work, thanks to your coaching. You can also discover their beliefs and change.

<u>Necessity/discipline/clarity:</u> Players need some time to understand the exercise. There's a necessity.

<u>Learning transfer:</u> Holistic, all skills, your explanation, and coaching work like amplifiers.

<u>Your coaching (focused on defending):</u> What is the goal of defending? Preventing a goal against. From which part of the field can the opponent score? Around our goal (in our box), that's where they are not allowed to come. The opponent wants to get to our goal. How often do they succeed? A number of times. With whom and where on the pitch do they often succeed? They often switch sides so that the back has space to dribble across the center strip. Who can solve this? The attackers or the defenders? The attackers are being outplayed. What else can they do to prevent the opponent from going through the dribble back to our half? Have the attackers position themselves lower so that they are less likely to be played out by a switch of sides. And if they force the opponent to play the ball to their right back, they must avoid the side change. How are you going to do that? Our right-winger has to move on inwards when their right-back has the ball. He's with their left back but should be more between their left center back and left back. Then the right back kicks the ball long because of pressure from our left-winger, or he plays the ball back to their goalkeeper without being

able to switch sides. The defenders must then be extra sharp for a possible long ball. Do you recognize the connection between this exercise and the competition? Yes, we're pressing the opponents whilst they're building up.

CH#7
COACHING A MATCH

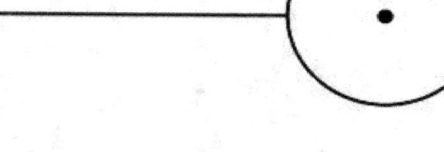

How Do You Make A Difference?

In the match, it comes down to it – or not – what's more important, winning or learning? In this chapter, I will go through the question of what it is actually about for you, your players, and the fans. Your answer to this question determines your approach. Who are you lining up? What do you say during half-time? In short: How do you make, as a coach, the difference?

> **Winning is fun. Sure, but winning is not the point.**

Pat Summitt

The Coach Makes the Difference

How do you make a difference when coaching a match? I might say a lot about it, but the words of the former basketball player and coach Pat Summitt, fit in well with my vision:

"Winning is fun. Sure. But winning is not the point. Wanting to win is the point. Not giving up is the point. Never being satisfied with what you've done is the point. Never letting up is the point. Never letting anyone down is the point. Play-to-win, sure. But lose like a champion. It's not winning that counts. What counts is trying."

Another thing I'd like to add here is a quote from Bobby Knight, a former basketball coach as well:

"The key is not the will to win. Everybody has that. It is the will to prepare to win that's important."

CH#7 - Coaching A Match

7.1 Wanting To Win

- The Aim Of The Game?

"Whether you win or lose, you can always grow."

-Ali B

A few years ago, I spoke with Joshua Brenet when he was still playing in PSV 1. At the time, Brenet was the PSV player with the record of the longest run of matches being unbeaten in PSV1. PSV were champions a few times during that period in the Netherlands, so in our conversation, winning was a hot topic. He told me that with PSV, only winning matters. Yet I had a pressing question to which I couldn't predict his answer a hundred percent.

"Joshua, I want to present to you two scenarios for next season, as if we could look into the future. Scenario one is that PSV become champions. Great for the club, but you play little or nothing. Scenario two is that you play everything, you develop yourself, and therefore you might attract attention from other clubs. Only with PSV, you do not become champion, but you finish second or third. For which of the two scenarios do you choose?"

Of course, it's hypothetical, but I was very curious to what extent winning is the most important thing at the highest level in the Netherlands. What do you think he chose? What would you choose? What would your players choose?

Consequences of the Focus on Winning

Every player, every team, and every coach wants to win and wants to do a lot for that to happen. You play a game to win, that's one of the reasons why you train. But at the same time, I think almost everyone has experienced the negative sides of a focus on winning in youth can have.

Coaches from various sports at home and abroad have expressed their concerns about the focus on winning in youth divisions. The American Valerie Kondos Field is one of them. Kondos Field was a ballet dancer and has been a Gymnastics coach at the University of California Los Angeles for over thirty-five years. Both as a dancer and as a coach, she has won many prizes, including even the award of 'coach of the century.' In her Ted Talk, however, she states that in the youth, a hyper-focus on winning prevails. Winning must happen at the cost of everything. Kondos Field won many youth competitions with her youthful athletes but got a so-called wake-up call from them. Her athletes labelled her as a commander who determined everything, even bullying her athletes. What she wanted had to happen, and her athletes had to conform to it. Her athletes wanted to win, naturally, but not in this way; because of this, they lost their fun in sport, even the best athletes did. Some of them became depressed, burnt out, and or decided to quit the sport they loved doing so much. Kondos Field then decided to change course. From now on, she coached her athletes on their intrinsic motivation and spent time getting to know the person behind the athlete. The consequence? The athletes still won youth competitions, but now with much more fun.

In his book *Late Bloomers*, Karlgaard writes that the increased focus on being the best, and preferably as young as possible, creates tensions, fears, and unhappy feelings among young people from all walks of life in society. In fact, in recent decades, depression amongst adolescents has increased fivefold worldwide, making it the number one cause of illness and disability in teenagers. Is that the future we want to offer our youth?

CH#7 - Coaching A Match

I have experienced the consequences of this focus on winning or having to be the best in youth with soccer players, but now also outside of football. I have been a teacher in higher education since the summer of 2020. In my role as a teacher, I also mentor/coach students. After the first test period, a student wanted to talk to me. She experienced a lot of stress because of her test results.

The first thing she tells me is that she doubts herself, "I wonder if I can do it. Am I good enough for this study? Or should I do something else?"

I indicate that I like her approaching me and sharing her doubts with me. She then briefly explains that these doubts cause her stress, and she experiences little rest or relaxation.

"What grades did you get?" I ask her.

"One 7 (out of 10) and furthermore all passings," she responds.

"You passed all the courses?" I ask to check. She answers affirmative.

"You know you pass the study and get your diploma when you pass all your subjects, right?" She knew that, of course.

But what turned out? She doubted herself and experienced stress because she wasn't topping the class. Her confidence, and her sense of success, had little to do with her passing the subjects, but especially with comparing her performance with that of other students. That means she always has to be the best for herself to feel good. In previous years, she succeeded in this, but this study is one step up, and the group to compare herself with has grown. Then there is a good chance that someone else will get better points than her.

"What is your goal with this study?" I asked her.

"I want to get my degree," she said.

"Do you think the grades of other students play a role in whether you get your diploma?" She thought not.

"Does your diploma increase in value if you get the best grades? Or will your diploma decrease if you get the lowest pass of everyone?' She knew that wasn't the case."

In the further course of the conversation and coaching her, I continued to focus on her own trajectory. Ultimately, she set herself a completely controllable goal, and since then, she has experienced more peace and relaxation.

Basically, there is nothing wrong with comparing yourself to others or wanting to do everything well. It can even be motivating. But it gets dangerous if you can't accept you are not the best or don't do things at the best level, and this directly affects your confidence or self-esteem. This can lead you into thinking the best matter, and the rest does not. That kind of thought and goal, I think, is a result of the hyper focus on winning and is probably not so helpful for performance and learning. Social media may play a role in this too. How can you help players who feel they only matter if they are the best, do everything perfectly or win the match? Help them focus on their task and their own influence. Please read chapter 3.2.

- *If winning is more important than anything else, you run the risk of getting players to lose their motivation and thus, fun.*

Is Winning Important For Youth Players?

Of course, you can always ask your players what makes them tick, but research has shown why children play sports. Wanting to win is one reason but not the most important one. These are the reasons why children play sports:

1. Doing their best.

2. Being treated with respect by their coaches.

3. Playtime

4. Playing together in a team and getting along well with teammates or even friends.

5. Being busy and trying things.

...

48. Win.

What many young athletes, and also youth soccer players in the Netherlands, struggle with has also been studied. These are the reasons why they lose fun in doing sports:

1. Continuous assessment or performance pressure (from coaches and/or parents).

2. Not enough playing time.

3. Afraid of making mistakes.

4. Sport-social balance (side jobs, doing homework, et cetera).

Which scenario did professional football player and record holder Joshua Brenet choose in the end? Becoming a champion, but playing hardly or not at all? Or scenario two; play a lot of matches but not become champions? He chose scenario two! He chose to play and not become a champion. Logically, that's what (most) youth players also opt for.

Mark Tuitert, former speed skater and Olympic gold medalist, tells in one of his *Drive* podcasts that many top athletes think they are happy after winning a match. These top athletes are disappointed because it often doesn't work that way. Tuitert says you don't necessarily have to be happy by winning a match. He states that you should be happy with what you do, that's the basics. From that, you strive for goals, such as winning matches.

Mikaela Shiffrin, being hosted by Dr. Michael Gervais in his *Finding Mastery* podcast, talks about this too. Shiffrin is an alpine skier and has won a total of 14 medals during Olympic Winter Games and World Cups. Among those 14 there's 8 gold medals. Shiffrin said that winning is fun, sure. However that winning feeling lasts only one second. What about the rest of the time you're practicing and preparing? You either have to enjoy that or find something else to do.

In another *Finding Mastery* episode Paul Annacone, who coached tennis stars like Pete Sampras and Roger Federer, tells Dr. Michael Gervais young tennis players should seek fulfillment in more than just winning. After all, there's only one winner at every tournament, so the rest has to find another reason(s) for being there.

What applies to you? How important do you find winning a youth match? What are other ways to feel fulfilled next to winning?

- *Youthful soccer players want to win but find other matters more important. Things like respect, being allowed to participate during a match, and doing their best.*

Is Winning Important To Coaches?

Years ago, Johan Cruijff gave his view on the role of winning in a youth academy at Pauw & Witteman's talk show. He said, "There is only one team that has to win within a soccer club, and that is the first team. But an academy has nothing to do with winning. For them winning is only a small part. An academy is all about improving your qualities. Then you grow, and then you get to the first team and then it is mandatory to win."

Youth is all about developing. Winning is not the most important; that's the tenor of Cruijff's ideas. Almost everyone will agree with that. Cruijff put this into practice by positioning players in different positions during the match. Thus, the player became forced to develop certain skills and to learn to think from a different position.

"When a player with possibilities could not defend, I let him play in defense to learn, but that sometimes costs a point." Dennis Bergkamp is perhaps the best-known example. "When Bergkamp broke through at Ajax as a right winger, he had played as a right back for two months. Bergkamp was positioned right back because he outplayed his opposing left back too little as a right winger. So he had to learn how a left-back thinks. That's what he learned as right back." Cruijff saw a youth match as a moment to perform, but perhaps even more as a moment to develop soccer players through play.

However, also, for some coaches of first teams in professional soccer, development seems to be more important than winning. Juanma Lillo, mentor to Pep Guardiola, in an interview, said, "The objective is the journey and the process; the work you put in, matters. Do you go into a soccer stadium in the last minute of a game and have a look at the scoreboard and leave? You watch ninety minutes of the game, which is the process. What enriches you is the game, not the result. The result is a piece of data. Fulfillment comes from the process." Louis van Gaal wrote in his book, *Visie*, 'Actually it is not about the results, it's about the quality of the play. The end goal is to improve the quality of the game.' And obviously, the better the quality of the play, the bigger the chance is to win.

The Coach Makes the Difference

But why is it that some coaches have certain players not play for a minute on Saturdays, are early maturers overrepresented in selections, and does the relative age effect exist? Because it can be extremely important for a club and/or coach to win. First of all, winning is great; it makes you feel good and nourishes the ego. Secondly, as a coach, you want to be or appear competent. You get to deal with other coaches, with parents who sometimes seem to have invented the game too, and other people with opinions about you as a coach. You want to come across as a good coach with them. Winning youth matches can contribute to that. It gives you status. Third, you can view winning youth matches as a measure of your players' development. Determining your players' development is difficult, but a match's result is simple and clear. So, the more youth matches you win, the better your players may develop. Finally, the effect of professional soccer on youth soccer is not to be underestimated. The soccer that everyone sees on television is played by the pros. The professional soccer world is a world where winning can dictate the difference between being champions and bringing in sponsors and money, and finally, between having a job or being unemployed. That ensures that many clubs and coaches are driven by the short term; they have to win now. That image influences our view of youth soccer. In comparison, the world of youth soccer is different from the professional world.

- *Winning gives a good feeling and status. Winning seems like a measure of development, but it is not by definition. Our vision of winning is influenced by professional soccer/sports, but we have to realize that in the professional world, it is all about results, and in the youth, it is about development.*

The Difference Between Winning And Developing

Are winning and developing really that different? Yes, fundamentally different. If you want to win, you have to avoid mistakes. Your players can best take as few risks as possible. For example, they almost only play with their favorite foot, hardly build up or not at all, but kick the ball forward, and you, as a coach, give especially the best players of today playing time and opportunities. The team must achieve results, and your players are subservient to them.

Development is about improving, and that comes with making mistakes. Your players will train skills they haven't mastered yet. This entails risks because there is a real chance that it will go wrong. But, your players, for example, play more with both right and left foot, find the soccer solution, and you give all your players playing time and opportunities. The team strives for results, with every player getting chances to improve his performance.

- *Winning is about the short-term goal; meanwhile, development is about the long-term.*

Why is it not useful to always focus on the short term when you're busy developing? Because that comes at the expense of opportunities for and the development of young players. Of course, you can teach your team how to defend, but have them defend in their own half for a season long, so to only prevent the opponent from scoring is something else. These teams are only working on stopping the opponent, and if they win the ball once, they immediately kick a long ball in the hope their players up front will eventually win a sprint duel and score. But what do your players

The Coach Makes the Difference

learn when you have such a way of playing all season? For example, are your midfielders getting better at unmarking and playmaking?

It can be a tactical idea, or sometimes you can't help it, like when your team is struggling with injuries. But some coaches go into matches purely for the win and throw all the skills and intentions they have been training with their players overboard. That's a shame.

The short-term and long-term bite each other, and in my opinion, it's a matter of time before performance improvement in the long term catches up with performance in the short term. But it's up to every club and each coach to determine what they stand for in this area. I have to always think of a statement by Pieter van den Hoogenband: 'A performance based on chance has no value.'

- *Think carefully about whether you want short-term or long-term results. With the focus on winning, you achieve the first, with the focus on developing the second.*

What Is Your Vision On Winning?

When asked how important winning is, I got different answers from the youth academies of Liverpool and Real Madrid. At Real Madrid, winning is all that matters. With every team, they want to be the best, from their youngest youth team up to their first team. They constantly search in each age category for the best players to win. They're aware of the relative age effect and shrug their shoulders. Youth players at Real Madrid are subordinate to the appearance of the club. Being the best is what they want to radiate.

At Liverpool, they indicated that winning with youth teams is important, but developing their youth players is most important.

Some clubs and coaches have the same vision as Real Madrid; others resonate more with Liverpool. In addition, there are clubs and coaches who seem to have no idea what is more important to them, winning or developing.

There are players who, from a young age, are looking for the pressure to win. Those players thrive on that. On the other hand, are players – in my experience, that is the largest group – who thrive better on the view that winning is important, but their development is most important. At a later age, and especially at the higher levels, the pressure of having to win is increasing. Most players grow up to that in a natural way; they learn to deal with it better and better because it suits their age and development.

What it starts with for you as a coach is that you clearly know what you stand for. Is winning the most important thing for you, or is developing all your players? Express this so you give players and their parents a chance to determine whether your perspective and associated behavior suit them.

What do I choose? I like to win, but in an academy, I find performing and developing to be much more important. For me, performance means a player is the best version of himself on the pitch. By this, I mean that he can be himself without doubts or distractions, so his focus is completely on his game, and as a consequence, he plays to the best of his abilities.

The Coach Makes the Difference

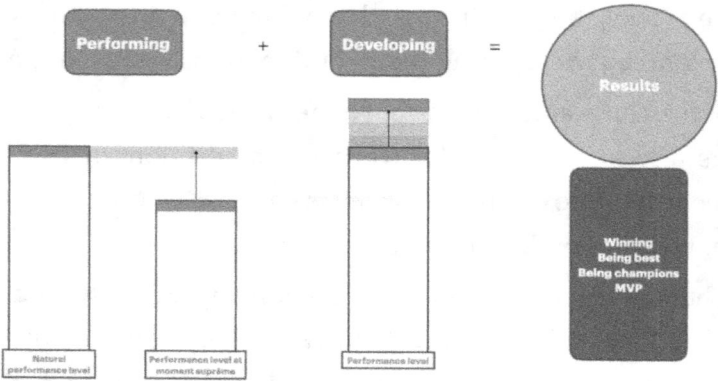

Besides that, I want to improve his performance and raise the bar of his goals because long-term development is what I think it's all about for youth players. The better they develop, the better their performance is. And the better their performance, the more likely they are to contribute to winning matches, both at a young age and as an adult.

How Kobe Bryant views winning and losing is inspiring to me. His answer to the question "What does losing do with you?" might be different from what you'd expect.

Check out his answer via the 'Chapter 7.1 Kobe Bryant' link at https://www.bauer-vandelooij.nl/bijlage-boek.

I think it's fantastic that my players want to win, but we win on two conditions: We win together, and every player gets playing time and opportunities to perform and develop themselves. We win with the way we play; we play soccer the way we want and train.

CH#7 - Coaching A Match

With my Willem II team, we had agreed on three values as the golden standard within our way of play. We mirrored the players' behavior after every game (and training) to this golden standard. These three values became slogans, and I believe most players will remember them when they are eighteen. They relate to guts, collaboration, and perseverance. We always wanted to see that. Moreover, those values shaped our chosen tactics and individual tasks in matches.

Stan van Gundy, a former professional basketball coach, makes you think with this fired up talk on the role of winning. Check it out at: https://www.bauer-vandelooij.nl/bijlage-boek.

> • *Winning says something about the relationship between you and your opponents. Performance says something about you compared to yourself. Performing is achieving goals and pushing your own limits so that you grow and develop.*

Summary

Winning has several aspects to take into account in your focus as a coach:

With a focus on winning comes the risk of demotivation and less fun.

For most children, wanting to win is not the main reason why they play sports.

A focus on winning is about short-term results, and a focus on development is about performing and developing in the long term.

Determine your own vision of winning and it's importance, and make sure your club and players think alike.

7.2 Safety

- Can everything be there?

   "The fact is that people are good, give people affection and security, and they will give affection and be secure in their feelings and their behavior."

   -Abraham Maslow

On Thursday evening, June 12, 2014, a few players from the Dutch National Team have trouble falling asleep. Tomorrow is the first group match of the World Cup. Even though these players have played many matches on top level and thus are quite experienced, they feel tense up to the point they can't sleep. Is that weird? Is that wrong? I don't assume any of these things. Research has shown competition does have such an effect on people, and it stays there whether you're a rookie, have some experience, or even if you have played more than 500 games. The tension does not disappear. However, you can learn to deal with it differently.

These Dutch National Team players – and your players, too – have emotions and feelings, such as tension, anger, or joy. Emotions and feelings are not wrong; they're part of the game whether you like it or not. So the question is not how a player gets rid of it; it's there to stay. The question is, 'How does the player deal with it? And what can you do to help the player deal with it?'

A sense of safety helps your players perform at their best. They should not be in (life) danger when they step onto the pitch because then their focus and energy are mainly on survival rather than playing soccer. That's why matches are moved to other areas when this safety isn't guaranteed because of war or a pandemic. In addition, it helps your players when they feel psychologically safe.

The Coach Makes the Difference

Then, within the rules of the game and team agreements, they can be themselves and do what they think is right. That sense of safety allows your player to focus and spend his energy completely on the match so that he performs what he is capable of.

> Research done by Amy Edmondson, Vanessa Druskat, and Julia Rozovsky has shown psychological safety to be the distinguishing factor between top teams and good teams in intensive care units and Google, among others.

What Can You Do To Help Your Players Feel Safe?

As a coach, you can contribute to a safe environment.

First, ensure predictability. Hardly anyone likes insecurity. Not knowing what to expect or what will happen is often not pleasant and can cost a lot of energy. In your pre-meeting, tell your players what you expect from them. Come back to what you trained and give your players information about the opponent, if possible. Predictability is extra important if you have a difficult message for a player. For example, are you planning to bench a player after he has been in the starting lineup for weeks? That is, of course, not a nice message to give and for the player to receive. Maybe he disagrees. That's okay, and you don't have to agree. But it is good to prepare him for the message. For example, tell him after the last training session or before the team meeting. Then he has time to let it sink in, so his reaction during the team meeting will be different. Provide predictability.

Secondly, you can do your best to have everyone on the team feel they are accepted and they belong. Dutch professional men's field hockey team Bloemendaal has been quite successful lately with winning three championship titles in a row and their 22nd in total in 2022. They ascribe their success to the fact that everyone feels accepted in the team. What did they do? They were not only doing things together on the pitch but also off the pitch, so they got to know the person behind the player by having something to eat or drink together. One of the biggest mistakes leaders make when it comes to psychological safety and having team members feel they belong is that they not only tend not to ask questions, but when they do, they tend to answer their own questions without listening to their team members. To what extent does a team member feel he and his vision belong? Daniel Goleman, an authority on social and emotional intelligence, said on this specific topic that by asking questions and listening to the answers from team members, you not only involve others, but you also get to know them, how they see things, and what drives them. They then feel they matter to you as a leader, and they feel that they belong. On top of that, listening to team members gives you valuable information in striving for team and individual goals. More on how to connect with one another, having everyone feel they belong, and getting to know the person behind the player is written in chapter 2.4, Relatedness.

A third thing you can do to create safety is to empathize with the other. Be aware of the fact that everyone has their difficulties, doubts, or problems, and make sure you are there for him during those times. The emotions of your players, however different, may be there. You want to help them deal with that. Do you find that difficult? Then think about how you have ever felt and behaved when you were not at your best. Did you (then) never need and benefit from another person's understanding?

"You get frustrated on the pitch. What's it like to play like that?'

"You've been out of shape lately. How are you?'

"You just can't seem to score. What does that do to you?"

Also, think about your behavior during the match. How do you think players feel when you're freaking out at the sideline every time they fail at something?

Psychiatrist Steve Peters, who's worked with Team SKY and Liverpool FC amongst others, says it is sometimes necessary for your emotional part of the brain, which he calls the Chimp, to speak freely about your emotions. Just let it have a go. In this way your rational part of the brain, which he calls the Human, gets to listen and eventually will come up with a solution or the insight that you might just be a bit too emotional. But at least then there's been space for your emotions and to process them. So for you as a coach sometimes it's wiser to let your players vent their emotions and just listen. Either listening is enough, they will feel freed up, or you get to play the rational part in the story by coming up with a solution or put things in perspective.

Simon Sinek calls this 'empathy'. He sees empathy as an important quality of a leader. Empathy is the ability to be in tune with others.

Watch the video via the link 'Chapter 7.2 Simon Sinek' at https://www.bauer-vandelooij.nl/bijlage-boek.

With my first team at PSV, we played a nice two-day tournament in Germany with appealing opponents. On the first day, the team performed well and achieved good results. We had qualified for the Champions League group whilst ending up in the Europa League in the year before. That was wonderful for my players. So we wanted to continue on the second day. We played against an opponent that is normally better than us. But my players gave everything, went through hell for each other, and we played soccer as we had trained. Just before the final time, we were 2-1 down in a fairly even game. A draw was the correct reflection of the game. With just a few seconds left, we attacked one more time, and our striker got the ball at his feet in front of an open goal. He got the 2-2 on a silver platter. But he shot the ball just wide! Some boys fell on the ground in disappointment, and the referee whistled for the end. What a disappointment for all of us.

I called the players together. When they came walking up to me, I saw some players talk in frustration and accuse our striker for losing this match. He was the scapegoat in the eyes of his teammates. My striker guiltily walked my way with tears in his eyes. I remember how disappointed I was then because I granted my team so much to get a good result in this match. Once they were with me, I told the team that this sucks, working so hard with each other and playing so well and then missing such a great opportunity just before time. The disappointment made sense. At the same time, we couldn't stay in this too long, because we were going to play more games that day. In addition, it was important that my striker could get this match over with so he could play the next games feeling free.

"Men, our striker obviously missed the chance at 2:2. Now look at him."

The boys looked at him, somewhat frustrated, and he broke down.

"You're really bummed. I can see that. I hear that from what you say. But what would our striker feel? How bad will he feel? Right now, I am going to ask something of you that is very difficult. In this moment, our striker needs you and your support more than ever. He really didn't miss on purpose, he did his best, just like you. And just like you, he sometimes misses too. I want to ask you to support him. If you can do that, if he feels that you are there for him, he is more likely to score again in the next matches."

While I was speaking, some players walked up to our striker and gave him a hug or put their arms around him. The striker gave me a look I will never forget. He was new that season and from Germany and might have expected me to be mad at him. His tears had dried up, and instead of sadness or fear, he looked at me with a certain determination.

Do you have to accept everything and turn off all your emotions? No, of course not. Do what you feel and think is right. But be aware of your behavior and its effect on your players. What almost always works well is to radiate peace and tranquility. Move calmly, talk calmly, and stand firm but relaxed.

The Danger of Suppressing Emotions

Stories from (former) professional soccer players show the importance of dealing with emotions. Among others, Gregory Van der Wiel, who has played more than two hundred matches for Ajax and Paris Saint-Germain, among others, says he has always experienced pressure but suppressed his emotions, such as anger, frustration, and sadness. He experienced the consequences during his time with Paris Saint-Germain (2012-2016), where he didn't feel happy. He didn't get the real bill presented until 2019 in the form of panic attacks. Those have been holding him back from a return on the pitch.

Sander Aarts, Netherlands' best-trained soldier, tells in the *Drive* (podcast) that he and other soldiers had learned to put

CH#7 - Coaching A Match

theiremotions aside or turn them off. His experience is that it is not possible; sooner or later, the emotions will rise.

Summary

Safety is about 'being allowed to be who you are.'
1 Accept what your players feel and experience.
2 A player feels safe if he knows: what is there may be and there are always solutions.
3 You create safety in your team by being predictable, and empathic and help your players learn to deal with their emotions.

7.3 Vulnerability

- Can I be imperfect?

> *"For the strength of the pack is the wolf, and the strength of the wolf is the pack."*
>
> -Rudyard Kipling

I played a friendly match during the week with my team. After I told the team goals, the same ones we trained on that week, the players got changed, and I went outside to prepare the warming up with my assistant coach. During preparation, a player who was upset came to us, tears streaming down his cheeks, "Why am I right back? I do not want that. I can't!' In order to guarantee his anonymity, I refer to him with 'right back' instead of his name.

It emerged from the conversation with him that this boy was afraid to make mistakes. He was new to our team that season and, of course, had to get used to the new situation. That's logically not something to happen overnight; it is an adapting process that can be quite exciting and takes time. That night the prospect of him having to play against the opponent's left winger was the straw that broke the camel's back.

"I know the left winger. He's the best player on that team," said my right back.

After a chat with my right back and my assistant coach, we went to the changing room. I knew his fellow players had seen him go out, and upon entering, they noticed his tearful face.

It was clear what I had to do.

The Coach Makes the Difference

"My dear friends, you have seen that our right back was crying. He thinks it's quite exciting to play tonight and actually feels so in being part of our team and academy. Can you imagine that?"

A 'yes' rang out from several corners of the locker room. Some players even shared their own experiences, "When I started in the academy, I also found it super exciting."

"Okay, so we can imagine. It's nothing crazy; that tension belongs to it. Tension also prepares your body and brain for a fight; it makes you alert. Anyway, besides being our right back today, he has also been a scout for us. He told us that the opponent's left winger is their best player. How are we going to make sure we help our right back so that the left winger is not tonight's best player?"

Fingers shot into the air.

"We'll back him up."

"We will coach him."

"Great ideas. About the backing him up: which player can best give him cover?'

The team indicated: the right center-back.

"Okay, guys, two more things. First of all, our right-back agreed an individual goal for tonight with our assistant coach. He wants to win one duel with his direct opponent. You can help him in the pitch by coaching him. Finally, suppose it doesn't work out, and our right back loses a duel or loses a ball. What can we then do to help him? You can ask him, " Right back, what do you like?"

Our right-back was now a bit more upright, his tears were dried up, and his eyes widened, probably from surprise and relief. The team was there for him, especially when he was so vulnerable. Together with his fellow players, he discussed the coaching in case of mistakes or when he would not succeed.

How did the match go for him? Our right-back won his first duel with the left-winger in the very first minute, who was hardly dangerous in the first half. Three or four teammates coached him during the first half and complimented him when he won his duels. Our right back, in total, won more than nine duels to both the left winger and other opponents in that first half.

These situations of tension and uncertainty are more common. On any level and at any age, a player or coach can feel vulnerable. That's part of it. You're being vulnerable when you dare to indicate that you have doubts, don't know, or can't do something yet. But in doing so, you are actually very powerful and brave.

- *As a coach, you want your players to be open to learning. Them showing their vulnerability helps with that. A player who thinks he can do everything already, who dismisses every mistake or blames others, is not what you'd want. But a player who is being vulnerable opens doors to performance and development.*

How Do You Respond To Vulnerability?

To be vulnerable, your player needs courage. You and his teammates play an important role in whether he dares to do so. You can divide your behavior in roughly three categories: you behave unhelpfully, you act helpful and supportive, or you ignore your player and his vulnerability.

Burning, laughing, blaming, and embarrassing him are examples of unhelpful behavior. You do this often, and no one dares to be vulnerable anymore. The atmosphere within the group? Mistakes are indeed made, but always by someone else. Players start blaming each other and hide their own failures.

Ignoring speaks for itself; you pay no attention to the player and leave his vulnerability unanswered. This ensures that players are not going to feel safe and free with you. It's at the expense of your bond with your players, and their performance will not be optimal.

With helpful behavior, you open up vulnerability, you acknowledge the player and what he is dealing with, and you let everyone know it's okay to be vulnerable.

- *At any level and at any age, a player or coach can feel vulnerable. By opening up and supporting, you open the door to development. In addition, you show everyone is allowed to be vulnerable.*

Set a Good Example

Vulnerability starts with the leader, with you as a coach. That also takes courage from you. Because you show that you don't know everything and cannot see or do everything. You show that you are human, which again creates a bond with your players. They see that you are doing your best but that you are sometimes wrong. Just like them.

We played a friendly practice match against another professional academy team. We did not play in two halves but in four quarters. After a good first quarter, I felt we were a bit less in the second quarter. We had to run after the ball more than we wanted to. It annoyed me, and I let my players know.

"In the first quarter, we had the ball. We dominated the game. But who was in control the in the second quarter?"

"We!" The players shouted, quite in unison.

CH#7 - Coaching A Match

This came as a total surprise to me. I replied in a rather firm way, "No, definitely not. They were in control in the second quarter. We mainly ran after the ball."

A day after the match, I watched the video of the match, and I saw that my boys were right. In the second quarter, our team played well again; we were in control. I had been wrong. Between quarters one and two, I coached my strikers in how to put pressure. They weren't too smart in doing so, so they had to run a lot. In the second quarter, them putting pressure was lacking wits. My focus was too much on the attackers and their lousy way of putting pressure; that's where my feeling came from. When I realized that, I decided to address the group in the next training session.

"Boys, I have watched the match on video, and you were right. In the second quarter, we were better and in control, like you said. At that time, I was convinced we were not in control and was a bit firm with you. I shouldn't have. I got it wrong. So you see, I – or the staff – aren't always right either. So always think critically and form your own vision."

Klopp explains how he sees vulnerability and shows it during an interview, "If I expect from myself that I know everything and can do everything, I wouldn't have self-confidence. Because I know, I'm good at some things, very good at a few things, and that gives me confidence. That's why I'm able to grow others around me. What I consider important is that I am empathetic to the people around me and that I really try to understand them and support them in what they do. That's leadership for me: making sure the people around me can do their thing.

Klopp's advice is, "Don't act as if you know and can do everything, but make sure you have good people around you who are more knowledgeable than you in certain areas. Be willing to admit it if you don't know something. Tell you have to look it up and get back to it!"

In the soccer world, and perhaps also in your working world, vulnerability is often seen as a weakness. It is seen as a sign that you are not good enough. As far as I'm concerned, that's a narrow-minded thought fitting a fixed mindset. That thought makes it hard to be vulnerable, while being vulnerable actually amplifies your connection with your players, other coaches, and colleagues. They might even want to help you out. Finally, they probably follow your lead.

Everything nice and all good, you may think, but can you perform with that vulnerability? The following example proves you can.

Bayern Munich is one of the world's largest soccer clubs. But, at the beginning of November 2019, the club is not running at full speed. They were not topping the league table, and internally there were doubts about players like Neuer and Müller. Was it time for fresh blood? Because the club sacked head coach Kovač, and has not yet reached an agreement with one of the ideal candidates, their assistant coach, Hans-Dieter Flick, was promoted to head coach temporarily. Almost a year later, Flick won 35 of 38 matches with Bayern Munich as well as the Bundesliga, German Cup, Champions League, and European Supercup, with the eye-catching 8-2 victory over FC Barcelona. Under him, the players revived. In August 2020, The New York Times wrote an article about this German trainer. What was his secret?

Players who have experienced Flick as an (assistant) coach share their take. Flick is characterized as a socially competent trainer who behaves humbly, takes time for his players, listens to them and takes their doubts seriously, and also removes them. He just says the right thing at the right moments. What makes Flick so good, and maybe is his secret, is that he dares to be vulnerable. His vulnerability leads to vulnerability in his players.

Funny detail: Flick formed the coaching duo for years with Joachim Löw with the German national team that became world champion in 2014. They were the first coaches duo of the German team without having played a single international match played for the German national team.

> Jordan Henderson, who's been captain of Liverpool FC for a long time, speaks about being vulnerable with Jake Humphrey and Damian Hughes' *High Performance* podcast. Henderson says the best thing you can do is to open up to other people if there's things troubling you. Talking about them helps. So open up yourself if needed, but also be aware some of your players might need to open up and you can offer them a sympathetic ear.

Here's two quotes from Brené Brown, the authority on vulnerability, for you to think about:
'Vulnerability is not winning or losing; it's having the courage to show up and be seen when we have no control over the outcome. Vulnerability is not weakness; it's our greatest measure of courage.'
And:
'Daring leaders work to make sure people can be themselves and feel a sense of belonging.'

- *Be vulnerable and create an atmosphere in which your players also dare to be vulnerable. It provides more connection and increases the chance of better performance, development, and results.*

The Coach Makes the Difference

Summary

Accept and acknowledge that you or your players don't know or can't do something.

Vulnerability is not a weakness; it's a strength. It opens doors to development.

Create an atmosphere in which players dare to be vulnerable.

Give a good example yourself.

7.4 Goal Orientation

- What am I fighting for?

"If you don't know which port you're sailing to, no wind direction is favorable."

- Seneca

A match is about scoring more goals than the opponent. You have to go to the opponent's box to score and at the same time, defend your own goal to avoid conceding goals. In a 1v1 duel, the task and results of your player's behavior are clearly visible. He alone is responsible for the goals he scores and concedes; he can't blame teammates. Soccer is a team sport in which the team achieves a result; the team wins or loses a match. Your players are responsible as a team and need each other. Messi also needs his teammates. Messi has, to my knowledge, never taken the goal kick and outplayed all opponents without passing the ball before scoring a goal. Because you achieve results as a team, you have to work together. But what if one of your players has not clear what his task is?

After a U14 match, our defensive midfielder came to me. He wanted to reflect on his performance after every game, which I applaud. This leads to, among other things, insight into the cause-effect relationships of his performance.

"Did I play a good game?" the player asked me.

I bounced the question back and asked him for his opinion.

He wasn't sure. As a team, they scored a couple of goals, but he had not scored or given any assists. He, therefore, thought he hadn't performed very well.

The Coach Makes the Difference

This is a logical thought for many players. Goals, assists, or fouls through which the opponent scores are clearly discernible. The whole team is responsible for the goals, but each player has his own task, so I asked him about his task in the field.

"In defense, I have to make sure the ball stays away from our goal by closing the passing lines or intercepting a pass. In attacking, I have to assist or score."

I was pleased with his answer, that he shared his view. I could do something with that.

"If you think you should be involved in a goal on offense, then what are the tasks of the other players? For example, what are the tasks of our defenders? Do they also have to assist or score for a good performance? What then is the task of the attackers as midfielders have the task of scoring?"

He didn't know very well. So I explained to him how we wanted to play, building up from the back and passing from zone to zone to reach the opponent's goal.

"Do you know what your task is in that? What is your task in build-up?" I asked.

Then the penny began to drop. He said it was his role to get the ball from the defenders to the midfielders or attackers. Or at least, getting the ball higher up the field toward the opponent's goal because a defender or himself could also dribble in. So it was up to him to unmark in such a way that he could receive the ball in midfield by a pass from the defender or that he makes room for the defender to dribble into the midfield.

"How many times have we managed to build up?" I asked.

After thinking for a while, he indicated that we had succeeded quite often.

"What was the most successful way, through a pass or a dribble?"

"A dribble from the defender. I helped him by luring my opponent with me; this gave the defender the space to to dribble in."

I concluded with the rhetorical question: "Did you perform well in attack then?"

It would have been even stronger if I had stats about our build-up and his behavior in that.

Set team goals per game

Because football is a team sport, your players share the responsibility for the result. Of course, every player can assist or score a goal, gladly even, but in principle, every player has his own specific role with a specific task, matching his position on the field. The task of an attacker is to score goals. The task of the goalkeeper and defender is: to prevent the opponent from scoring goals. The task of a midfielder is: connecting with defending and attacking. This requires other skills and behavior per position. With team goals, you can set match goals, such as scoring goals or preventing them, more concretely at both team and individual levels.

When defending, a team goal can be: force the opponent to kick a long blind ball forward. Which players play a role in this? Who does what and when? How do we work together on this? What does that mean for you in your position?

When attacking, a team goal can be: in the build-up, we want to get the ball in midfield. Who plays a role in this? Who does what and when? How do we work together on this? What does that mean for you in your position?

The Coach Makes the Difference

It helps to let players think before the game or even come up with a plan. The players agree on how and what they want and take more responsibility on the pitch. You monitor whether the team goals are achieved. These stats provide direction, motivation, and self-confidence. And if you ask your players how the statistics came about, they also help your players understand the game better. Such a statistic can be: the opponent came in our box five times, or we had one chance with a header from three corners.

* *Setting team goals and discussing them together can make a match goal more concrete and clarify the role of each individual player.*

Set Individual Match Goals

From team goals, you can set individual goals. Well-stated individual goals give your players even more direction and can help them maintain their focus on their task on the pitch.

Examples of common individual goals are: winning one duel with my direct opponent, passing the ball forward, dribbling past my direct opponent five times, and scoring two goals.

The great thing about these goals is that your player's intention is clear. The danger of these goals is that they become goals in themselves.

Suppose your player's goal is to pass his opponent five times in the first half. What if, after forty minutes of playing, he's only succeeded once? He can continuously, in any situation, look for the second, third, fourth, and fifth chances to pass his opponent so that he can achieve his goal for the first half. But what if his opponent has cover from two of his teammates? Then dribbling past the defender with two players covering him is not the best choice. And that, making the best choice in every situation, is what distinguishes top players from good players.

So, the intention of the stated goal is a good start, but the wording could be better.

A better goal in the example above is: if you are 1v1 and there is space then you dribble past your direct opponent 75 percent of the time. If that specific situation only occurs four times, the goal is to dribble past opponent three times.

With such a goal, you teach your player to recognize the situation and make a (best) choice. This demands a lot from you as a coach. Maybe you have a staff so you can divide the individual goals among your staff? Substitutes, team managers and physiotherapists often love to pay attention to the individual and team goals, is my experience. However, maybe I can count myself lucky with the staff that I had.

- *Formulate an individual goal that fits well with the team goal. Don't let the goal become an end in itself. That's how you stimulate the player in recognizing situations, making choices and acting towards his goal.*

Be aware of the dichotomy of control

Finally, what is important to take into account when setting goals, is the dichotomy of control (see chapter 3.2). "I want to score two goals" is a different goal than "I want to radiate energy for forty-five minutes". In the first goal, there's factors your player doesn't control, such as the game plan or the quality of the opponent, but also whether his fellow players see him and pass the ball to him in favorable situations. It is not a fully controllable goal.

The second goal is a fully controllable goal, because only your player can influence whether he radiates energy for forty-five minutes. He can't control not what happens on the pitch, but he can control how he reacts. Does he leave his head hanging to the ground or does he go for it? This is a completely controllable goal for him.

You can connect the different types of goals with each other though. Suppose your striker's goal is to score two goals. What is he going do to increase that chance? Peel it off until it's a fully controllable goal. Maybe it comes down to something like: I'm in the box whenever we attack that area. He probably won't always get loose from his man-mark, get into a firing position or get the ball, but being in the box with every attack does help him. If he isn't in the box, then your striker knows that the chances of scoring are very slim. The only one who basically determines whether he is in the penalty area during an attack, is your striker himself. The more often he gets there the bigger the chance he will score his two goals.

Perhaps the best goal is a so-called infinite goal. An infinite goal is a goal that has no end point, but continues to exist like "I give my very best in every situation." A finite goal is a defined goal with clear criteria, such as 'I want to score two goals in forty-five minutes'. A disadvantage of a finite goal is that it can demotivate the player if he fails a few times and the goal seems unfeasible. What if his goal is 'I keep unmarking around the box?' Then the player has a new chance to achieve his goal every time again, even if he failed previous times, and that motivates. That's the big advantage of an infinite goal.

- *Your players can always achieve a fully controllable goal, because they have hundred percent influence on that. They are hundred percent responsible for the success. Achieving a fully controllable goal provides confidence and motivation while increasing the chances of success with incompletely controllable goals.*

The Coach Makes the Difference

Summary

If you make match goals concrete, you increase your chances of winning.

Set team goals and make sure every player knows how he can contribute to them.

Set individual goals.

Set fully controllable goals.

> **Leaders become great, not because of their power, but because of their ability to empower others**

John Maxwell

7.5 Timing

- What do you say when?

> *"A tongue may weigh little, but can crush a man."*
>
> -Chinese Proverb

Your players perform at their best when they are 'free'. By that, I mean your players are themselves. They don't walk around with doubts, questions, or other distractions but are fully focused on playing soccer. Their belief in their own abilities plays a major role in this because the stronger your players believe they are going to perform well or even believe they are going to win the match, the more likely they are. Because from that belief come actions aligned with that belief.

Before and during the match, you can influence the performance of your players. You do this in advance with a pre-match meeting, during the match, you coach along the line, and during half-time you give a halftime talk. Just as soccer has many facets, there are many ways in which you can influence your players.

You can focus on the tactical plan, on the technical execution, on team and individual goals, or you can inspire your players with a story. What do you say and when? Do you discuss tactics in advance, or do you want to inspire your players? Do you give your players technical tips during the match? Do you remind them of the goals? Do you compliment your players or give them the proverbial kick in the ass? Only you can answer these questions. After all, you know your players best, and you estimate what helps them the most. Helping them can be difficult; for example, I sometimes gave a way too long pre-meeting so that half of my players fell almost asleep.

My goal was and is to stimulate my players' belief in their abilities. In it, I experimented with many ways of pre-match talks. From saying nothing at all to telling in great detail what everyone in his position had to do, from giving responsibility to the players to telling a story. Those last two ways worked best in my experience. A story often contains a message that players take with them on the pitch. The power of a good story is that it is emotionally appealing. In giving responsibility, I positioned myself as a coach. "What do you want in defense? What do you want in attack? How are you going to do that? Make plans in groups."

In addition, consider whether all your players need the same thing. Find out what each of your players individually helps to deliver the best performance. Maybe you can discuss certain tactical matters with the main characters and set goals with the players who need them. Who knows, you might discover it is better to leave some players alone.

Whatever you do, in my experience, it works best to coach on the things you trained. If you've trained on technique, it's crazy if you suddenly coach on tactical matters during the match.

Finally, think about your use of words because words have the power to change the brain. Also, your words. You can be negative or positive using words; both have a different effect. Generally, negative words activate the fear center, the amygdala, of your players. This leads to fear, irritation, and a reduced ability to logical reasoning, and it leads to a release of stress hormones that are bad for the brain. Above all, it reduces your players having fun, at least for most players. Do you want to address the motivation center of your players? Then use positive words. That leads to more motivation, believing in your own abilities, creativity, and resilience in your players.

I once asked my players what stimulated them. Their answers seemed different, but with further questions, it boiled down to the same thing: they all wanted to hear the truth, as far as my view is the truth. Truth can be hard, but even then, you can send your message in a negative or positive way. Negative is that you tell the player that he is underperforming, and he will keep doing so. No player is waiting for that. Besides, you don't know whether that's true. A player who is underperforming now may, in the (immediate) future, perform better. I think that's positivity.

Negative Words	Positive Words
"You're only good as a substitute."	"You can do it, I believe in you."
"You are of no use at all."	"I'm not asking for perfection. I ask you to do your very best."
"If this is how you play, then you're on the bench for the rest of the game."	"Go for your chance."
"You're having a hard time. I don't see how you'll do better."	"You're having a hard time. But I trust you can do better."

"It's been rubbish this first half. Playing the second half makes no sense."	"It's been rubbish this first half. Luckily there's a second half to show how good we are."
"What a disgrace today. I don't know how to turn this around in training sessions."	"What a disgrace today. Let's get to work in training sessions to improve ourselves."

Table 9 • Examples of Negative and Positive Word Use

Positivity doesn't mean to me that you just accept everything and think all is good, while you're not good at all, or if it just isn't positive. You give the players your (hard) reality and leave open what the future brings. Possibly you tell the player that he can influence his future with his behavior. Because I believe development is possible, I often tell my players I believe they can improve in the future. Players are waiting for that, I have experienced.

Current Benfica and former PSV Eindhoven coach Roger Schmidt seems to work like this with his players. After scoring against FC Utrecht on Sunday, December 13th, then PSV-player Mohamed Ihattaren runs into the arms of his coach Schmidt. Ihattaren had not had a top season so far, did not play much after the arrival of Schmidt at PSV, and Ihattaren even got sent away from a training session by the German coach.

The Coach Makes the Difference

"The coach has been very tough. And fair too. I have to give my hundred percent. Also, outside the pitch." Schmidt states that one of his tasks is to develop young players. "If things go less well or with difficulty, you have to tell them the truth sometimes. Sometimes you have to indicate that they are on the wrong road and have to change their behavior." According to Ihattaren, Schmidt was hard and fair, but the coach remained positive by saying that he saw Ihattaren's qualities last season. "Show that too in my time as coach," he told me.

Do you have a player who needs a 'hard' approach because, for example, he acts uninterested, or do you want to excite a player? Give him responsibility and use his ambitious goals. Mirror his behavior to that responsibility and that ambitious goal. That works best in my experience.

- *By being honest and positive, you stimulate intrinsic motivation and belief in your players' own abilities. Find out what every individual player needs for his best possible match performance and help him with that.*

Summary

What do you say during a match?

Coach on what you have been training.

Align with what the player needs in the moment.

Positive words have a better effect than negative words on your players' intrinsic motivation, believe in own abilities and match performance.

CH#8

How Do You Bring The Ideas And Tips From This Book In Your Practice?

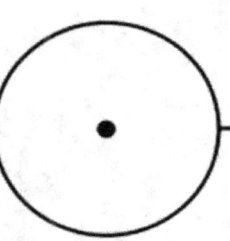

HOW do you become a coach who makes a difference? That's a process of falling and getting up, just like playing soccer. Have a critical look at your approach but be gentle at the same time. Allow yourself time to develop. Because you know: you're only going to see when you get it. In this chapter, I'll give you some handy tips. Let me reveal the most important already: be yourself.

Tips. The most important I reveal in advance: be yourself.

> **If you haven't learned the lessons to bring them into practice, what did you learn them for?**

Epictetus

You have almost reached the end of this book. I hope I have made you think about your role as a coach and you are (extra) inspired to make a difference for your players. Now it's on you to apply the tips from this book in a way that suits you. Form your own opinion and vision based on what you know now. Let these seven insights that follow help you with this.

Insight 1 – Learning is done by trial and error

Don't expect everything to go right all at once. That didn't happen to me, and I don't think it happened to anyone. Because, as a coach, you work with people, not with, for example, math problems, to which often only one answer is the correct one. In working with people, there are always several ways to handle or solve the same situation or problem. Sometimes you don't know exactly which way works or how you can best approach something; that's part of the deal. It would even be crazy if you did know and did do so all the time. That would probably be boring too.

I've often been at my wits' end because I didn't know how to handle a particular player or given situation. And I still have that now and then, even after those years as a coach in a professional academy. In fact, I think it'll be like that. That's not always fun, sometimes even frustrating, but above all, challenging. It taught me a lot about developing and interacting with others.

In addition, the effect of your progress as a trainer is not always immediately visible. If you change your feedback from person to specific behavior, it does not suddenly lead to much better players, performance, or results in the next match. It's not a one-to-one relationship, because multiple factors play a role, like time. Therefore, focus as much as possible on your behavior. How do you want to behave? Stick to that, and success, whatever your definition may be, will come naturally.

Insight 2 – Your development takes time

My tips may be new to you or different from what you're used to do. Because you probably have developed ideas about behavior or habits that are normal for you. You may now be working on that. That can feel weird and unnatural, and that makes sense. In fact, that's a feature of your brain. Your habits are ingrained in your brain and cost you little effort to do. It flows relatively unconsciously, and that is efficient. Learning new behaviors makes you aware of what you are doing, and that costs energy. Once the new behavior has become a habit, it's going to feel normal. As players learn to improve their behavior and performance on the pitch with trial and error, so do coaches develop themselves too.

Insight 3 – Learn from others

When I started at PSV, I had zero experience as a coach, and I had to discover and learn the coaching profession entirely. That was, certainly, in the beginning, with falling and rising. In addition to delving into books about soccer tactics and coaching and attending presentations, I was just about lucky to have the best possible learning experience. There were a lot of coaches at PSV with years of experience and knowledge from whom I learned a lot. I'm probably not completely objective, but with Bastiaan Riemersma as a mentor, I was blown away. He taught me so much in such a short time about being a coach. I felt that I learned from the best. That didn't go in a 'soft' way. Bastiaan was demanding; he saw me in half after training sessions. That was quite spicy at times because I really did my best on the pitch, but the bar had to be raised. At the same time, he supported me by asking questions and by giving me advice. Gradually the sawing became less, and the coach in me got better. In my opinion, Bastiaan is one of the few coaches and heads of the youth academy that really believes in development. That shines through, sometimes against the radical, in his vision and behavior, as with my appointment at PSV. Besides Bastiaan, I have benefited a lot from the coaching conversations with Toon Gerbrands, the general manager of PSV at the time. He made me think hard about leadership and mirrored my behavior to my words and vice versa. Also, Roger Bongaerts and Mark Huis in 't Veld helped me on my way when I was just starting out as a coach.

I have experienced that you are not a good coach in an instant. However, I do believe anyone can become a good one. It helps if you have people around you that support you, make you think, and act as a mirror of your words and actions. Read a book or listen to a podcast. Those are all things you can do to become a better coach.

Be open-minded. Be open to your players. What do they think? Be open to other coaches. What are their experiences? Be open to new realities; for example, do you believe in development? Be open to changes. Do you stay informed? Be open to your own development. How do you deal with feedback? Be open to other perspectives and people as much as possible so that you become the best possible coach you can be.

Insight 4 – You don't have to be good at everything

You may feel empowered by what players, probably yours too, appreciate in a coach. For your players, you don't need to be the new Guardiola with the latest tactical ideas. Your players don't need you to know everything about football technique. You don't need to win all matches to be loved by them.

Players appreciate you when you give them the opportunity (read: playing time), everyone at his own level, to deliver their best performance on the pitch. Players appreciate you when you look out for them and are there for them. Players appreciate you if you are genuinely interested in them as a person and not only as a soccer player. Players appreciate you if you are friendly to them. Players appreciate you if you don't take yourself and soccer too seriously, and you offer room for humor to also have a laugh with each other. All in all, your players appreciate you if they feel you want the best for each of them. With that positive intention, you will eventually find the solution for every situation, every problem, and every player. I'm convinced of that. What if you don't find it? Keep looking, then at least your players will feel that you do your very best for them. What more can your players wish?

I find what Klopp says about this inspiring. See the video 'Chapter 8 Jürgen Klopp' via the link on

<https://www.bauer-vandelooij.nl/bijlage-boek>.

Insight 5 – The principles in this book apply to all ages and levels

Are there no differences in terms of age or level, do you ask? I can already hear you thinking: thank you for this book, but I don't deal with a player of nine years old in the same way as I would with a player at age nineteen. Looking at the tips in this book, I say: in principle you do. Of course, in general, a player of nineteen years old is further developed physically, cognitively, and social-emotionally than a nine-year-old player. That's why you can expect more from older players. For example, they understand more difficult words and can think more abstractly about tactics. They are physically capable of more, such as giving a pass of 40 meters through the air. Older players are ahead in their development, so that, for example, they can better see the consequences of the match results and are better able to deal with pressure, like having to win. These are some examples in which age causes differences. The same goes for the soccer level. In general, you may expect more from players who are active at a higher level than from players who play at a lower level. Yet there are also many similarities. Just think about the following questions:

- Is intrinsic motivation for playing soccer less important for a nine-year-old than for a nineteen year old?

- Would a nine-year-old want to be part of the team, but a nineteen-year-old wouldn't?

- Are they both happy with their coach's genuine interest in their person?

- Do they both like enthusiasm from their coach?

- Can they both appreciate fair treatment from their coach?

- Do they prefer a coach who communicates succinctly on the pitch so that they can play soccer a lot, or would one prefer a college by his coach and play much less football?

- Is working together in a soccer team only important for a nineteen-year-old, or also for a nine-year-old?

The guidelines in this book apply to every age and at every football level, in my experience.

Insight 6 – Adjust your approach to what boys and girls need.

"Do I treat a girl the same way as a boy?" is a question I got asked while writing this book. Honesty bids me to say I'm not the best person to answer this question. I haven't worked much with girls on the pitch. Luckily know a few coaches who know more about this, and I spoke to some of them. Based on what they told me, I dare say the guidelines in this book apply just as much to girls as they do to boys. Still, there are a few things to keep in mind.

Girls, in general, are more relationship-oriented than guys. That's not to say the relationship is more important to them, it is for boys just as important, but a girl is more concerned with it. Where a boy may not always be waiting for a conversation when it comes to soccer, this is more often the case with a girl. They chat or, as one player put it, like to 'bicker' with each other. So have lots of conversations with your girls about soccer. Because girls are more relationship-oriented than guys, they can find it hard to give and receive feedback and might have issues in leadership. In particular, they don't want to harm each other. Help them in this by keeping the goal in mind and indicating that they are being coached on their behavior. At the same time, girls often want to know more about the exercise and ask for feedback more. Do you have a team that consists mainly of boys and only one or a couple of girls? Discuss at the beginning of the season with your players what the season will look like. Ask them – just like the boys – for their wishes, also clearly indicate what you expect and act accordingly. If you don't? Then there is a good chance that you don't get it back from your girls immediately, but a few months afterward you will. By that time, the frustration has already risen considerably, and it is more difficult to turn. By the way, the girls I spoke to enjoyed playing soccer with boys. Often the level with boys is higher, which means girls are challenged. From the age of fifteen, however, the challenge becomes too big because many boys then become physically stronger and better at playing soccer too. Most girls can't go with that.

Both coaches and girls I spoke to had to think long and hard about the differences between boys and girls. That means, to me, that differences between boys and girls are not so much at the group level but rather on an individual level. Because, like boys, girls need autonomy, competence, and connectedness. They, too, perform better if they have a stronger belief in their own abilities. Girls also prefer a coach who cares about them, who is friendly and doesn't take himself too seriously. The guidelines in this book apply, therefore, to both boys and girls.

Insight 7 – Everyone is unique

Finally, soccer is for everyone. Therefore, realize that every player on your team is different. Every player is unique. The background, the development, the qualities, and the ambition of your players differ from each other. Those differences are not scary or wrong. Your players don't all have to be the same or be equally good. As long as you have the same goal, the differences strengthen the team. Get to know the person behind the player and find out what works and what doesn't work for every individual player, and take that into account in your interaction with him or her. The better your relationship with the individual player (perhaps most importantly), the greater the chance that he or she will perform and develop optimally. Get started, in short, by connecting with their intrinsic motivation and their belief in their own abilities. Then you

The Coach Makes the Difference

have come a long way already. Ultimately, every player, young or old, girl or boy, wants the same: to enjoy playing soccer.

> **None of us is as smart as all of us**

Ken Blanchard

The Coach Makes the Difference

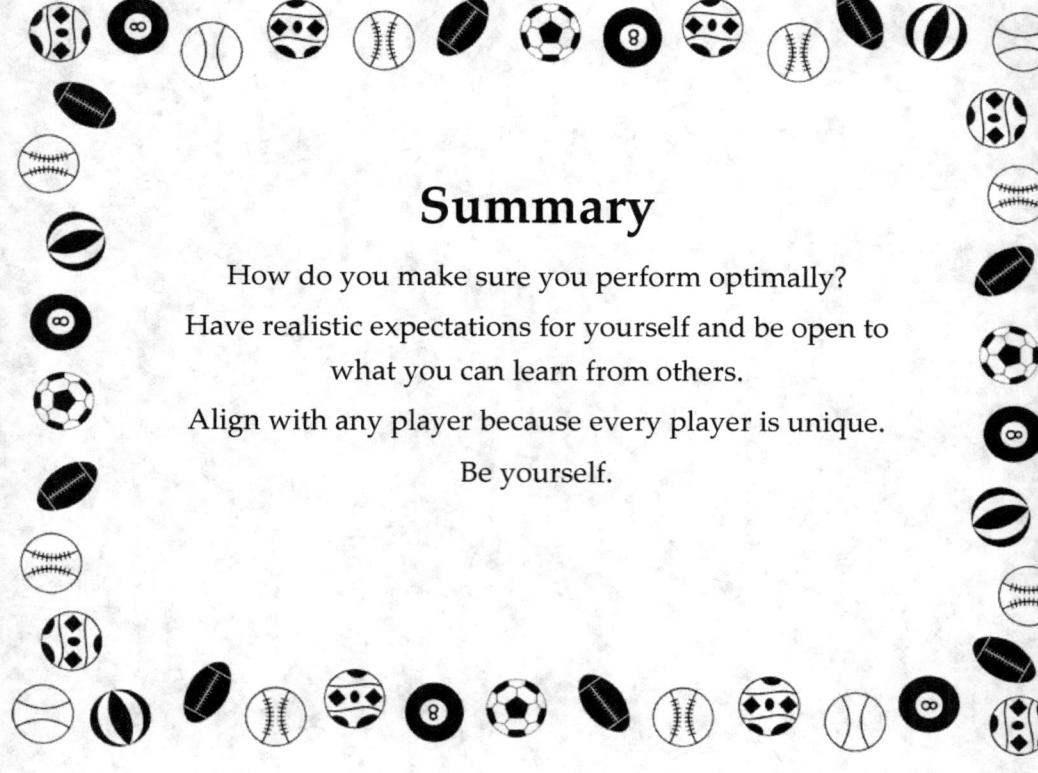

Summary

How do you make sure you perform optimally?

Have realistic expectations for yourself and be open to what you can learn from others.

Align with any player because every player is unique.

Be yourself.

Inspiring People, Book Tips and More

My goal was to write as clearly and smoothly as possible. Hence I have not put any references in the text but I have benefited a lot from the knowledge of others. And therefore I want to share their names and books with you here.

Do you want to learn more about leadership? Then I recommend the works of Stephen Covey and Simon Sinek.

In the field of intrinsic motivation, scientists Ryan and Deci are the authority. They have developed the prevailing theory of motivation. In the Netherlands, Dr Jacques van Rossum is an authority in this field; he can talk about it with enthusiasm.

I recommend Carol Dweck's books if you want to know more about the growth mindset. She's at the basis of this theory and has written about it in her book *Mindset*.

If you want to know more about the dichotomy of control, stoicism is an interesting philosophical movement to get to know better.

In terms of ownership, I have benefited a lot from the book Extreme Ownership of former Navy Seals Jocko Willink and Leif Babin. Also, the book *Niet Te Breken* by Sander Aarts, the best-trained soldier of the Netherlands, is a must. Roderick Göttgens makes you think about, among other things, (team) culture and collaboration with *Teamability*.

Steve Lawrence has researched the relative age effect and has possible solutions.

Professor Arne Gülich is a German scientist who does a lot of research on talent identification and academies. His work is worth it. His Australian colleague Gulbin also has gained a lot of knowledge from his research into talent. In addition, works by Joseph Baker and Jean Coté are worth reading.

Daniel Memmert is a German scientist who does a lot of research on creativity in soccer. If you want more depth in that area, I can recommend his work. Horst Wein has written soccer books with exercises that allow you to develop the creativity of players.

For popular science books on talent and performance, search for work by David Epstein, Geoffrey Colvin, and Daniel Coyle.

I also got to know a number of people with a lot of knowledge about training and performing in (youth) soccer. They are an inspiration to me as a coach/teacher. If you have a good story, they are prepared to share their ideas enthusiastically with you while enjoying a cup of coffee.

Bastiaan Riemersma is a football coach and thinker with a refreshing vision of recognizing and developing talent. He is one of the few in The Netherlands who has the courage to form an academy in a refreshing yet radically different way. He will light you with his drive and enthusiasm and also make you think.

Michiel de Hoog is a journalist who writes a lot about interesting topics and inspiring stories about youth soccer in The Netherlands and abroad.

If you are looking for good exercises for your training sessions and playing principles for your way of play, then Willem Weijs and Javier Rabanal are two coaches who have a great archive. They are constantly looking for and creating the best exercises, and they develop their own exercises.

Inspiring People, Book Tips And More

You don't have time for a cup of coffee, but do you want to practice exercises right away for tonight's training session? Then I recommend the training tool Rinus of the Dutch FA to: https://rinus.knvb.nl/.

If you want to better understand the latest tactics and trends in soccer or want to read a good match analysis, then I refer you on to Pieter Zwart.

Acknowledgements

Are you considering writing a book yourself, and are you looking for a publisher that gives you honest feedback and coaches you during the process? Then I can highly recommend Donald Suidman. I thank Donald for his belief in this book and his time and energy to develop my ideas into the book as it lies before you. Brenda van Dijk helped me on the level of editing. Thanks to her, this is a smoothly running-and logical story. She really connects with the content of your book and looks beyond just the text.

In getting this book translated in English and published worldwide I'd like to thank my team at Amazon Publishing Pros and Alex Nielsen, Liz Hales and Helen Cooper in particular.

I want to thank my family, and especially Ellen, Paul, Sandro, Noortje, Rochelle, Mia, Mariëtte, George, and Iris, for their love and support while writing this book. In addition, I am grateful for the following persons and for their involvement in the creation of my book:

Art Langeler, Aschwien Kandhai (The Connection Coach), Bastiaan Riemersma, Job Peeters, Mariëtte van Tuijl, Mark den Brok, Martijn Bauer, the girls from Young PSV Women, Michiel de Hoog, Pieter van den Broek, Ronald Onstenk, Rutger de Waard, Thijs van Esch, Toon Gerbrands and Willem Weijs.

Special thanks to Dennis Reus, Ian Taylor, Jacco Verhaeren, Madlene Amgarten, Mirelle van Rijbroek, and Remco Wortel for their effort and help with the English publication.

Finally, I would like to thank my colleagues at PSV Eindhoven, Willem II, vv DBS and Fontys HRM and Applied Psychology for their collaboration.

Acknowledgements

In particular, I want to thank Daan van Oudheusden, Edwin de Wijs, Jeremias Carlos David, Job Peeters, Kristof Albrecht, Leon Vlemmings, Lonneke Nuijten, Manuel van de Wal, Martijn Bauer, Niki Vaes, Paul Nuijten, Paul van Zwam, Remco Wortel, Rick de Rooij, Sanne van de Sande-Prince, Thijs Matla, and Toon Gerbrands. I am grateful to them for their energy, the opportunities I got from them, the talks, and the times they were a mirror. This made me think more carefully about identifying and developing (soccer) talent. I got a lot out of that.

If you, a player of yours, your team, or your organization needs coaching or advice in the field of talent development and performance, Martijn Bauer and I are happy to help you with our coaching agency *Bauer & Van de Looij*.

Resources

Aarts, S. (2019). Niet te breken: Word mentaal onverslaanbaar door de ervaringen en lessen van de Special Forces. Amsterdam, NL: Boekerij.

ArtofBrilliance (2019, 31 mei). Lessons in LEADERSHIP from Jurgen Klopp. Consulted December 17th 2020, van https://youtube.com/watch?v=4jWZVtkJdC0&ab_channel=ArtofBrilliance

Audi P. Risa P. (2013, 27 April). Juanma Lillo Interview - The Blizzard Issue One. Consulted July 23rd 2022, from https://issuu.com/73ladro/docs/the-blizzard-issue-one_page_55-64_juanma

Baker, J., Schorer, J. & Wattie, N. (2018). Compromising talent: issues in identifying and selecting talent in sport. Quest, 70(1), 48-63.

Baker, J., Wilson, S., Johnston, K., Dehghansai, N., Koenigsberg, A., De Vegt, S. & Wattie, N. (2020, 25 november). Talent research in sport 1990-2018: a scoping review. Frontiers in Psychology. doiI: https://doi.org/10.3389/fpsyg.2020.607710

Bailey, R. & Collins, D. (2013). The standard model of talent development and its discontents. Kinesiology Review, 2, 248-259.

Balague, G. (2012). Pep Guardiola: Another way of winning: The biography. Londen, ENG: Orion Publishing Group.

Bergen, P. van, Graham, L. & Sweller, N. (2020). Memories of positive and negative student-teacher relationships in students with and without disruptive behavior. School Psychology Review, 49(2), 178-194.

Breitbach, S., Tug, S. & Simon, P. (2014). Conventional and genetic talent identification in sports: will recent developments trace talent? Sports Medicine, 44(7), 4-17.

Brink, C. van den & Wieldraaijer, E. (2011). Ruwe diamanten: Talentontwikkeling in de sport. Deventer, NL: Dam Uitgeverij.

Butter, J.C. (2018). Het ongewenste kind: een reis door het ongewone leven van Cristiano Ronaldo. Tijdschrift Hard Gras, 120. Ambo Anthos.

Collins, D., Macnamara, A. & McCarthy, N. (2016, 28 september). Putting the bumps in the rocky road: optimizing the pathway to excellence. Frontiers in Psychology, doi: 10.3389fpsyg.2016.01482

Conn, D. (2017, 6 oktober). 'Football's biggest issue': the struggle facing boys rejected by academies. The Guardian. Consulted December 14th 2020, from https://www.theguardian.com/football/2017/oct/06/football-biggest-issue-boys-rejected-academies

Coyle, D. (2018). The culture code: The secrets of highly successful groups. New York, US: Random House Usa Inc.

Covey, S. (2008). De zeven eigenschappen van effectief leiderschap. Amsterdam, NL: Uitgeverij Business Contact.

Cumming, S.P., Smoll, F.L., Smith, R.E. & Grossbard, J.R. (2007). Is winning everything? The relative contributions of motivational climate and won-lost percentage in youth sports. Journal of Applied Sport Psychology, 19(3), 322-336.

Dalio, R. (2017). Principles. New York, US: Simon & Schuster.

Davids, K. & Araujo, D. (2019). Innate talent in sport: beware of an organismic asymmetry – comment on Baker & Wattie. Current Issues in Sport Science, 4, 1-4.

Deci, E.L., Koestner, R. & Ryan, R.M. (1999). A meta-analytic review of experiments examining the effect of extrinsic rewards on intrinsic motivation. Psychological Bulletin, 125(6), 627-668.

Deci, E.L. & Ryan, R.M. (2008). Self-determination theory: a macro theory of human motivation, development, and health. Canadian Psychology, 49(3), 182-185.

Dell, A. (Regisseur) (2019). Antoine Griezmann: champion du monde [Netflix]. Consulted December 12th 2020, from https://www.netflix.com/nl/

De Hoog, M. (2021, 4 August). De nieuwe bondscoach is een bescheiden mens (en nog vijf geheimen achter het succes van Louis van Gaal). De Correspondent. Consulted July 23rd 2022, from https://decorrespondent.nl/9777/de-nieuwe-bondscoach-is-een-bescheiden-mens-en-nog-vijf-geheimen-achter-het-succes-van-louis-van-gaal/863388929205-4bf12bd4

De Voetbaltrainer (2019, 14 september). Onderbouw betaald voetbal, certificering en externe scouting. Consulted February 16th 2021, from https://www.voetbaltrainer.nl/2019/09/14/onderbouw-betaald-voetbal-certificering-en-externe-scouting/

Di Domenico, S.I. & Ryan, R.M. (2017). The emerging neuroscience of intrinsic motivation: a new frontier in self-determination research. Frontiers in Human Neuroscience, 11, 1-14.

Dweck, C. (2012). Mindset: Changing the way you think to fulfill your potential. Londen, ENG: Robinson.

Duckworth, A. (2016). De grit factor: De kracht van passie en doorzettingsvermogen. Amsterdam, NL: A.W. Bruna Uitgevers

Duhigg, C. (2016, 25 February). What Google learned from its quest to build the perfect team: new research reveals surprising truths about why some work groups thrive and others falter. Consulted

July 23th 2022, from https://www.nytimes.com/2016/02/28/magazine/what-google-learned-from-its-quest-to-build-the-perfect-team.html

Edmondson, A.C. (2019). The fearless organization: creating psychological safety in the workplace for learning, innovation, and growth. New Jersey, US: John Wiley & Sons, Inc.

Elfrink, R. (2020, 13 december). Schmidt is kritisch en blij na zege van PSV op FC Utrecht: 'Het is leuk om een knuffel te krijgen'. Eindhovens Dagblad. Consulted December 14th 2020, from https://www.ed.nl/psv/schmidt-is-kritisch-en-blij-na-zege-van-psv-op-fc-utrecht-het-is-leukom-een-knuffel-te-krijgen~a0287632f/

Elfrink, R. (2020, 13 december). Mohamed Ihattaren bedankt Roger Schmidt: 'De trainer heeft me laten zien hoe het profleven eruit ziet'. Eindhovens Dagblad. Consulted December 14th 2020, from https://www.ed.nl/psv/mohamed-ihattaren-bedankt-roger-schmidt-de-trainerheeft-me-laten-zien-hoe-het-profleven-eruit-ziet~ac8f979b/

Giles, S. (2016, 15 maart). The most important leadership competencies, according to leaders around the world. Harvard Business Review. Consulted Januari 10th 2021, from https://hbr.org/2016/03/the-most-important-leadership-competencies-according-to-leaders-around-the-world

Gould, D. & Carson, S. (2014). Fun and Games? Myths Surrounding the Role of Youth Sports in Developing Olympic Champions. Youth Studies Australia, 23(1), 27-34.

Goleman, D. (2013). The focused leader: how effective executives direct their own and their organizations' attention. Harvard Business Review. https://hbr.org/2013/12/the-focused-leader

Goleman, D. (2020). Leadership that gets results. Harvard Business Review. Consulted January 10th 2021, from https://hbr.org/2000/03/leadership-that-gets-results

Göttgens, R. (2018). Teamability: Zo vorm je extreem gemotiveerde teams. Zaltbommel, NL: Uitgeverij Thema.

Gulbin, J., Weissensteiner, J.R., Oldenziel, K. & Gagné, F. (2010). A look through the rear view mirror: developmental experiences and insights of high performance athletes. Talent Development and Excellence,2(2),149-164.

Gulbin, J., Weissensteiner, J.R., Oldenziel, K. & Gagné, F. (2013). Patterns of performance development in elite athletes. European Journal of Sport Science, 13(6), 605-614.

Gullich, A. (2013). Selection, de-selection and progression in German football talent promotion. European Journal of Sport Science, 14(6),530-537.

Gullich, A. & Emrich, E. (2014). Considering long-term sustainability in the development of world class success. European Journal of Sport Science, 14(1), 383-397.

Gullich, A. (2016, maart). Talent identification and talent development with particular regard to soccer. Poster presented during International Symposium for MEXT Top Global University Project, Tokyo.

Gullich, A. & Cobley, S. (2017). On the efficacy of talent identification and talent development programmes. In: Routledge Handbook of Talent Identification and Development in Sport, chapter 7. Londen, ENG: Routledge.

Gullich, A. (2019). "Is early reliable tid possible? No. Is it necessary? No, it is not." National Youth Sports Institute. Consulted December 14th 2020, from http://www.nysi.org.sg/news-and-media/is-early-reliable-tidpossible-no-is-it-necessary-no-it-is-not-prof-dr-arne-gllich

Hack, W. (2020, 2 november). Paniekaanvallen houden Van der Wiel en Kishna van het veld: 'Ik kon er niet mee leven'. Algemeen Dagblad. Consulted December 14th 2020, from https://www.ad.nl/nederlands-voetbal/paniekaanvallen-houden-van-der-wiel-en-kishna-van-hetveld-ik-kon-er-niet-mee-leven~ad405ce1/

Hersey, P. (2014). Situationeel leidinggeven: Een op de praktijk gericht model om flexibel te kunnen inspelen op wisselende omstandigheden. Amsterdam, NL: Business Contact.

Honigstein, R. (2018). Bring the Noise: The Jurgen Klopp Story. New York, US: Nation Books.

Howe, M.J., Davidson, J.W. & Sloboda, J.A. (1998). Innate talents: reality or myth? Behavioral Brain Science, 21(3), 399-442.

Hyman, M. (2010, 31 januari). A survey of youth sports finds winning isn't the only thing. The New York Times. Consulted December 14th 2020, from https://www.nytimes.com/2010/01/31/sports/31youth.html

ICS Group (2017, 27 July). Goalcast Roger Federer. November 4th 2023.

Ibarra, H. & Scoular, A. (2019). The leader as coach: how to unleash innovation, energy and commitment. Harvard Business Review. Consulted January 10th 2021, van https://hbr.org/2019/11/the-leader-ascoach

Jackson, P. & Delehanty, H. (2015). Eleven rings: The legendary BVO coach sharers the secrets behind his leadership and success. Londen, ENG: Ebury Publishing.

Johnston, K. & Baker, J. (2020). Waste reduction strategies: factors affecting talent wastage and the efficacy of talent selection in sports. Front. Psychol. 10:2925. doi: 10.3389/fpsyg.2019.02925

Jiménez, M., Fernández-Navas, M., Alvero-Cruz, J.R., García-Romero, J., García-Coll, V., Rivilla, I. & Clemente-Suárez, V.J. (2019). Differences in psychoneuroendocrine stress responses of high-level swimmers depending on autocratic and democratic coaching style. International Journal of Environmental Research and Public Health, 16(24).

Jowett, S. & Cockerill, I.M. (2003). Olympic medallists' perspective of the

coach-athlete relationship. Psychology of Excerise and Sport, 4, 313-331.

Jowett, S. & Timson-Katchis, M. (2005). Social networks in sport: parental influence on the coach-athlete relationship. The Sport Psychologist, 19, 267-287.

Karlgaard, R. (2019). Late Bloomers: The power of patience in a world obsessed with early achievement. New York, US: Currency.

Kirschner, P.A., Claessens, L. & Raaijmakers, S. (2018). Op de schouders van reuzen. Didactiefonline.

Knipping, T. (2020, 22 november). Het geboortemaandeffect: zo oneerlijk is het Nederlandse voetbal. VI PRO. Consulted December 11th 2020, from https://www.vi.nl/pro/het geboortemaandeffect-zo-oneerlijk-is-het-nederlandse-voetbal/share/bab03f0562

KNVB (2017, 21 januari). Nieuwe wedstrijdvormen pupillen: vragen en antwoorden. Consulted Februari 11th 2021, from: https://www.knvb.nl/nieuws/amateurvoetbal/competitiezaken/23190/nieuwe-wedstrijdvormen-pupillen-vragen-en-antwoorden

Kolfschoten, R. van (2015). Hoe simpel wil je het hebben? Eigenzinnige lessen en spraakmakende anekdotes uit het topvoetbal van Raymond Verheijen. Amsterdam, NL: Uitgeverij de Kring.

Kondos Field, V. (2019). Valerie Kondos Field: Why winning doesn't always equal success [Videobestand]. Consulted December 14th 2020, from https://www.ted.com/talks valorie_kondos_field_why_winning_doesn_t_always_equal_success

Liverpool FC (2020, 5 juni). How Jürgen Klopp creaties a winning culture at LFC | Presented by Western Union. Consulted December 17th 2020, from https://youtube.com/watch?v=sxrl0FP8vno&ab_channel=LiverpoolFC

Lund Dean, K. & Forray, J.M. (2019). "Perception becomes reality": how our beliefs affect student learning outcomes. Journal of Management Education, 43(4), 323-329.

Logtenberg, H. (2018). De hand van van Gaal. Amsterdam, NL: Prometheus.

McCarthy, P.J. & Jones, M.V. (2007). A qualitative study of sport enjoyment in the sampling years. The Sport Psychologist, 21, 400-416.

Misset, R. (2019, 21 december). Teun Koopmeiners, de geboren leider van AZ. De Volkskrant. Consulted December 14th 2020, from https://www.volkskrant.nl/sport/teun-koopmeiners-de-geboren-leider-van-az~b6bae6f2/

Moser, J.S., Schroder, H.S., Heeter, C., Moran, T.P. & Lee, Y.H. (2011). Mind your errors: evidence for a neural mechanism linking growth mind-set to adaptive posterror adjustments. Psychological Science, 22(12), 484-489.

Newberg, A. & en Waldman, M.R. (2012). Words can change your brain: 12 conversation strategies to build trust, resolve conflict, and increase intimacy. New York, US: The Penguin Group.

Nieuwenhof, F. van den (2010). Hiddink: Dit is mijn wereld. Baarn, NL: Tirion Uitgevers.

Ostojic, S.M., Castagna, C., Calleja-Gonzalez, J., Jukic, I., Idrizovic, K. & Stojanovic, M. (2014). The biological age of 14-year-old boys and success in adult soccer: do early maturers predominate in the top-level game? Research in Sports Medicine, 22(4), 398-407.

Pauw & Witteman (2011). Johan Cruijff over de ruzie in de Ajax-top (deel 2) - Pauw & Witteman. Consulted December 17th 2020, van https://youtube.com/watchv=xG1LFf5I7Nw&ab_channel=Pauw%26Witteman

Pigliucci, M. & Lopez, G. (2019). Handboek voor de moderne stoïcijn: 52 oefeningen voor een evenwichtig leven. Utrecht, NL: Ten Have.

Planting, R. (2001). Leerschool Ajax. Amsterdam, NL: Thomas Rap Amsterdam.

Rees, T., Hardy, L., Gullich, A., Abernethy, B., Coté, J., Woodman, T., Montgomery, H., Laing, S. & Warr, C. (2016). The great british medalists project: A review of current knowledge on the development of the worlds' best sporting talent. Sports Medicine, 46(8), 1041-1058.

Rommers, N. & Rössler, R. (2019). Innate talent in sport: from theoretical concept to complex reality - comment on Baker & Wattie. Current Issues in Sport Science, 4, 1-3.

Rongen, F., McKenna, J., Cobley, S. & Till, K. (2018). Are youth sport talent identification and development systems necessary and healthy? Sports Medicine - Open, 4(18), 1-4.

Ryan, R.M. & Deci, E.L. (2000). Self-determination theory and the facilitation of intrinsic motivation, social development, and well-being. American Psychologist, 55(1), 68-78.

Schroder, H.S., Fisher, M.E., Lin, Y., Lo, S.L., Danovitch, J.H. & Moser, J.S. (2017). Neural evidence for enhanced attention to mistakes among school-aged children with a growth mindset. Developmental Cognitive Neuroscience, 24, 42-50.

Shindler, J., Jones, A., Williams, A.D., Taylor, C. & Cardenas, H. (2016). The school climate - student achievement connection: if we want achievement gains, we need to begin by improving the climate. Journal of School Administration Research and Development, 1(1), 9-16.

Siekman, S. & Van der Loo, H. (2020). Cruijffiaanse techniektraining: op goede of gespannen voet met de sportwetenschap? Sportgericht, 74(5), 44-48.

Sinek, S. (2019). The infinite game. Londen, ENG: Portfolio.

Smith, R. (2020, 14 augustus). How a personal touch revived Bayern Munich. The New York Times. Consulted December 14th 2020, van https://www.nytimes.com/2020/08/14/sports/soccer/bayern-barcelona-champions-league.html

SoccerNews (2020, 3 januari). Ferguson negeerde katers bij United: 'We hingen de clown uit'. Consulted February 16th 2021, from https://www.soccernews.nl/news/647548/ferguson-negeerde-katers-bij-united-we-hingen-de-clown-uit

TED (2009, 25 augustus). The puzzle of motivation | Dan Pink. Consulted February 16th 2021, from https://www.youtube.com/watch?v=rrkrvAUbU9Y&ab_channel=TED

Tiki Taka Touzani (2020, 30 oktober). Straatvoetballer Soufiane Touzani gaat langs bij Wesley Sneijder voor een een-tweetje met én zonder bal. Consulted December 17th 2020, from https://www.npo3.nl/tiki-taka-touzani/30-10-2020/VPWON_1323403

Universiteit van Amsterdam (2017). Van studiesucces naar talentontwikkeling van studenten en docenten: rapport studiesucces 2.0.

Van Dam, M. (2022, 29 may). Bloemendaal alwéér landskampioen: 'Er zit nul gif in dit elftal, alleen maar liefde'. Trouw. Consulted July 23rd 2022, from: https://www.trouw.nl/sport/bloemendaal-alweer-landskampioen-er-zit-nul-gif-in-dit-elftal-alleen-maar-liefde~ba68bf6e/?referrer=https%3A%2F%2Ft.co%2F#:~:text=Hockey-,Bloemendaal%20alw%C3%A9%C3%A9r%20landskampioen%3A%20'Er%20zit%20nul%20gif%20in,dit%20elftal%2C%20alleen%20maar%20liefde'&text=Dat%20hockeyclub%20Bloemendaal%20zaterdag%20de,uitleggen%20hoe%20bijzonder%20dat%20is

Vella, S.A., Oades, L.G. & Crowe, T.P. (2013). The relationship between coach leadership, the coach-athlete relationship, team success, and the positive developmental experiences of adolescent soccer players. Physical Education and Sport Pedagogy, 18(5), 549-561.

Visek, A.J., Achrati, S.M., Manning, H., McDonnel, K., Harris, B.S. & DiPietro, L. (2015). The fun integration theory: towards sustaining children and adolescents sport participation. Journal of Physical Activity and Health, 12(3), 424-433.

Vissers, W. (2020, 2 december). Dries Mertens: de kabouter is een grote meneer geworden. De Volkskrant. Consulted December 17th 2020, from https://www.volkskrant.nl/sport/dries-mertens-de-kabouter-is-een-grote-meneer-geworden~b962defe/

Wagenaar, F. & Te Bogt, A. (2020, 19 september). Coaches over grenzen in de topsport: 'De buitenwereld wordt bozer, de sporter zachter'. Algemeen Dagblad. Consulted December 14th 2020, from https://www.ad.nl/sport/coaches-over-grenzen-in-de-topsport-de-buitenwereldwordt-

bozer-de-sporter-zachter~aa79bb74/

Welch, B. (2020, 22 december). What is football intelligence and can players develop it? The Guardian. Consulted December 24th 2020, from https://www.theguardian.com/football/2020/dec/22/what-is-football-intelligence-can-players-develop-it#:~:text=%E2%80%9CFootball%

20intelligence%20is%20about%20being,the%20nuances%20of%20different%20systems.%E2%80%9D

Willink, J. & Babin, L. (2017). Extreme ownership: How U.S. navy seals lead and win. New York, US: St. Martin's Press.

Wooden, J. & Jamison, S. (1997). Wooden: A lifetime of observations and reflections on and off the court. Chicago, US: Contemporary Books Publishing Group.

Zhao, Q., Zhang, J. & Vance, K. (2013). Motivated or paralyzed? Individuals' beliefs about intelligence influence performance outcome of expecting rapid feedback. Learning and individual differences, 23, 168-171.

Zimmerman, B.J. (2000). Self-efficacy: an essential motive to learn. Contemporary educational psychology, 25, 82-91.

Zuffiano, A., Alessandri, G., Gerbino, M., Kanacri, B.P.L., Di Giunta, L., Milioni, M. & Caprara, G.V. (2013). Academic achievement: the unique contribution of self-efficacy beliefs in self-regulated learning beyond intelligence, personality traits, and self-esteem. Learning and individual differences, 23, 158-162.

PODCASTS

Andrew Huberman – The HubermanLab:
https://hubermanlab.com/

Chris Williamson - Modern Wisdom Podcast:
https://chriswillx.com/podcast/

Dr. Dan Abrahams - The Sport Psych Show:
https://thesportpsychshow.libsyn.com/

Dr. Michael Gervais – Finding mastery:
https://findingmastery.net/

Jake Humphrey & Damian Hughes - High Performance Podcast:
https://www.thehighperformancepodcast.com/

John O'Sullivan - Changing the Game Podcast:
https://changingthegameproject.com/category/podcast/

Simon Sinek – A bit of optimism: https://simonsinek.com/podcast

Steven Bartlett - The Diary of a CEO:
https://stevenbartlett.com/the-diary-of-a-ceo-podcast/

The Coach Makes the Difference

Keystep media - First person plural:
https://www.keystepmedia.com/first-person-plural/

www.ingramcontent.com/pod-product-compliance
Lightning Source LLC
Chambersburg PA
CBHW071301110526
44591CB00010B/733